Engineering

How the Six Simple Machines Support the World

CARLA MOONEY
Illustrated by Lex Cornell

Nomad Press

A division of Nomad Communications

10 9 8 7 6 5 4 3 2 1

Copyright © 2025 by Nomad Press. All rights reserved.

No part of this book may be reproduced in any form without permission in writing from the publisher, except by a reviewer who may quote brief passages in a review or **for limited educational use**. The trademark "Nomad Press" and the Nomad Press logo are trademarks of Nomad Communications, Inc.

This book was manufactured by Versa Press,
East Peoria, Illinois, United States

October 2025, Job #J25-04636
ISBN Softcover: 978-1-64741-147-3
ISBN Hardcover: 978-1-64741-144-2

Educational Consultant, Marla Conn

Questions regarding the ordering of this book should be addressed to
Nomad Press
PO Box 1036, Norwich, VT 05055
www.nomadpress.net

Printed in the United States

More Engineering & Technology Titles from Nomad Press!

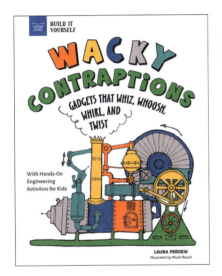 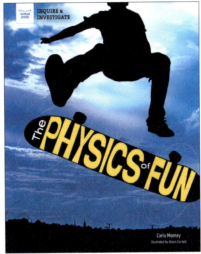 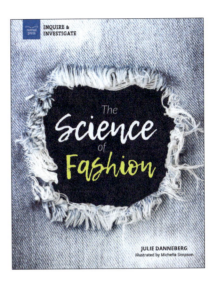

Check out more titles at www.nomadpress.net

You can use a smartphone or tablet app to scan the QR codes and explore more! Cover up neighboring QR codes to make sure you're scanning the right one. You can find a list of URLs on the Resources page.

If the QR code doesn't work, try searching the internet with the keyword prompts to find other helpful sources.

engineering

Contents

Timeline VI

Introduction
An Amazing Feat 1

Chapter 1
Inclined Planes 13

Chapter 2
Levers 27

Chapter 3
Pulleys 45

Chapter 4
Screws 59

Chapter 5
Wedges 75

Chapter 6
Wheels and Axles 87

Chapter 7
Putting It All Together 101

Glossary ▼ Resources ▼ Select Bibliography ▼ Index

TIMELINE

2.5 million years ago: Early humans use basic tools such as stone wedges for cutting and shaping.

3500 BCE: The wheel and axle are first used in Mesopotamia for pottery making.

3000 BCE: Ancient people use a long wooden lever called a shaduf to lift water.

2550 BCE: Egyptian Pharaoh Khufu orders the construction of the Great Pyramid to begin. Workers use the lever to move large stones for pyramid construction.

400 BCE: The first waterwheels and water mills are used to power machines in the Persian Empire.

312 BCE: Ancient Roman engineers begin the construction of a system of aqueducts that use inclined planes to carry water to cities and towns.

250 BCE: Archimedes develops the Archimedes's screw to move water from a lower level to a higher level.

73-74 CE: The Roman army builds a massive earth ramp to attack the Jewish fortress at Masada.

100: The first wheelbarrows appear in China during the Han Dynasty.

500 to 1000: Some of the first spinning wheels appear in India.

600: Windmills are used in the Middle East.

1100s: Gears are used in medieval clocks and later in other machines such as mills.

1400s: Leonardo da Vinci sketches designs for mechanical systems using simple machines.

1450: German inventor Johannes Gutenberg uses screws to build his printing press.

1500s: The use of gears expands in clocks, pumps, and other machines in Europe.

1687: Isaac Newton formulates his three laws of motion and gravity.

1700s: The steam engine is developed and uses multiple simple machines such as levers and pulleys.

1700s: The American pioneers use wedge-shaped axes and tools to split logs to build fences and buildings.

TIMELINE

1794: American inventor Eli Whitney patents the cotton gin, which uses a screw mechanism to separate cotton fibers and cotton seeds.

1804: British inventor Richard Trevithick builds a steam-powered locomotive, combining several simple machines.

1834: English mathematician Charles Babbage invents the analytical engine, which incorporates gears and levers as key components.

1850s: Engineers design elevators that use pulleys for lifting.

1858: American inventor John Landis Mason invents the Mason jar, a glass jar with a special screw-on lid that can be used to preserve food.

1888: The invention of air-filled tires makes rides smoother for vehicles.

1870s: American inventor Thomas Edison develops various devices using levers and gears in electric motors.

1893: George Ferris builds his Ferris wheel for the World's Fair in Chicago.

1914: The Panama Canal is completed with the help of pulleys and cranes.

1920s: Vehicles begin using steel wheels, which are stronger than wooden wheels.

1930s: American businessman Henry Phillips files a patent for the Phillips head screw.

1980s: Alloy wheels, which are lighter than steel wheels, make vehicles more fuel efficient and easier to control.

2000s: Modern machines, from cars to robots, rely on a combination of simple machines for efficient movement.

2002: Archaeologists discover the oldest known wooden wheel, the Ljubljana Marshes Wheel, in Slovenia. They estimate the ancient wheel is more than 5,000 years old.

2021: Amateur builders in China create the world's largest Rube Goldberg machine. It has 427 steps and lights a neon sign.

2025: Scientists and engineers are working to develop shape-changing wheels, also known as morphing wheels. These advanced wheels can change their shape to adapt to different surfaces or driving conditions.

TIMELINE VII

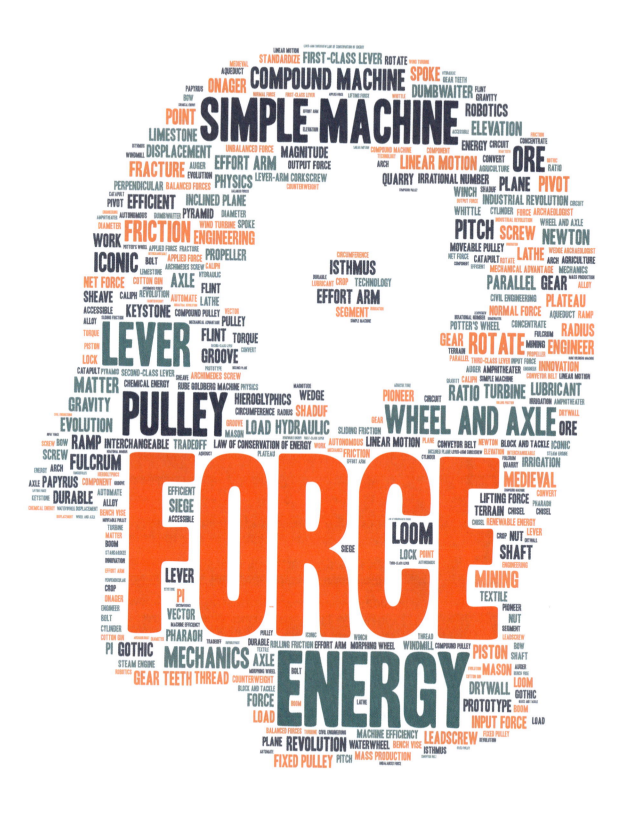

Introduction
An Amazing Feat

How do simple machines help us with engineering projects?

Since ancient times, engineers have used simple machines to build structures both large and small. The structure of our world—our homes, schools, bridges, monuments, skyscrapers, and more—is made possible by basic engineering concepts.

● ● ● ● ● ● ● ●

The Great Pyramid of Giza rises above a sandy plateau in northern Egypt. For more than 4,000 years, the Great Pyramid was the tallest structure in the world, initially reaching 481 feet tall. The Great Pyramid's base is a massive square. Each side stretches 756 feet across. The entire base covers 13 acres—that makes the Great Pyramid's base big enough to fit 10 football fields!

The Ancient Egyptians built magnificent pyramids as tombs for their kings, the pharaohs. The Egyptians believed that part of the pharaoh's spirit stayed with his body after death. They placed the pharaoh's body deep inside the pyramid, along with many items the pharaoh would need in the afterlife, such as treasures, jewels, and furniture. A series of mazes and dead-end passages inside the pyramid protected the pharaoh and his treasures. The entrance to the burial chamber was often blocked with heavy stone blocks or the burial shaft was filled so no one could get inside.

ENGINEERING | INTRODUCTION

The Egyptian Pharaoh Khufu (died c. 2566 BCE) ordered the construction of the Great Pyramid to begin around 2,550 BCE. Thousands of skilled workers, including stone masons and carpenters, came from communities throughout Ancient Egypt. They lived in a temporary city near the building site while they worked on the Great Pyramid.

The Ancient Egyptians used an estimated 2.3 million limestone and granite stone blocks to build the Great Pyramid. Most of the stone came from nearby quarries on the Giza plateau. Some stone came from quarries hundreds of miles away. Each block weighed an average of 2.5 tons, about 5,000 pounds. That's some pretty heavy building blocks!

Archaeologists believe the Egyptians used copper chisels to cut each stone to specific measurements. They placed the quarried stone on a wooden sled and pulled it to where it would be placed. Workers placed stone blocks in a square to form the pyramid's base.

How did the workers move the heavy stones to the pyramid's higher levels? Remember, they didn't have cranes or giant bulldozers. Without modern construction equipment, the stones would have been impossible to lift to the pyramid's highest points.

Instead, archaeologists believe the workers built sloping ramps to move the heavy stone blocks to the pyramid's next level. The sloping ramps were likely built from mud, wood, and stone. Workers pushed, pulled, and dragged stones up the ramps using ropes made from papyrus.

FULL STEAM

Two other significant pyramids were built at Giza, for Egyptian pharaohs Khafre and Menkaure.

THE SCIENTIFIC METHOD

The scientific method is the process scientists use to ask questions and find answers. Keep a science notebook to record your methods and observations during all the activities in this book. You can use a scientific method worksheet to organize your ideas and observations.

Question: What are we trying to find out? What problem are we trying to solve?

Research: What is already known about this topic?

Hypothesis: What do we think the answer will be?

Equipment: What supplies are we using?

Method: What procedure are we following?

Results: What happened and why?

AN AMAZING FEAT

Primary sources come from people who were eyewitnesses to events. They might write about the event, take videos, post messages, or record the sound of an event. For example, photographs are primary sources, taken at the time of the event. Watch out for fakes, though! Paintings of events are usually not primary sources since they were often painted after the event took place. They are secondary sources. Why do you think primary sources are important?

Workers may have greased the ramps with water or wet clay to make pulling the stone blocks on wooden sledges easier. They slid each stone block into place using wooden logs.

Workers placed the stone blocks in increasingly smaller squares, one layer on top of another. Once the stones were in place, the Egyptians used chisels to smooth the pyramid's sides and cover them with stone slabs. As each layer was completed, the workers built dirt ramps to the next level. Archaeologists estimate it took about 20 years to complete the Great Pyramid.

FULL STEAM

The Great Pyramid is so big it can be seen from the International Space Station!

4 ENGINEERING | INTRODUCTION

The Great Pyramid

AN AMAZING FEAT

Building the Great Pyramid was an amazing engineering feat. Ancient Egypt had no flatbed trucks to haul building materials or motorized cranes to lift heavy stones. There were no forklifts, power tools, cherry pickers, computers, or other machines that the modern construction industry uses to build everything from bridges to skyscrapers.

How did the Egyptians build one of the world's ancient architectural wonders without modern machinery?

Archaeologists believe the Egyptians accomplished this using simple machines!

Watch this feature-length PBS documentary to learn more about the Great Pyramid of Giza and how it was built. **Why did Egyptian rulers decide on this shape for their monuments?**

PBS Decoding Great Pyramid

A skateboard ramp is an inclined plane, one of the simple machines. A wheel is a simple machine, too!

For example, the large ramps built around the pyramid to move the massive stone blocks into place are a simple machine called an inclined plane. Pushing an object up an inclined plane is easier than lifting it. The Ancient Egyptians could move large stone blocks over great distances with simple machines. Building the Great Pyramid might not have been possible without the inclined plan.

WHAT ARE SIMPLE MACHINES?

Every day, humans perform work. Work can be as simple as mowing the lawn or as complex as building an airplane.

Throughout history, humans have invented tools to make work easier. Many human tools are based on simple machines.

A simple machine is a device that has no or few moving parts. Simple machines make work easier. They helped the Ancient Egyptians split massive rocks, lift heavy stones, and move materials long distances. With a simple machine, less force is needed to do the work. That makes the work easier!

There are simple machines all around us, from tools at home to machines worldwide. A wheelchair ramp is an example of a common simple machine called an inclined plane. You can push the wheelchair up the ramp instead of carrying it over the stairs. The ramp makes it easier to move the wheelchair to a higher elevation.

Two or more simple machines can work together to form a compound machine. For example, a wheelbarrow is a compound machine. It combines two simple machines: a lever and a wheel and axle. A shovel is another compound machine made from a lever and a wedge.

WHAT IS WORK?

To understand simple machines, we first need to understand the concept of work. Work occurs when a force acts on an object and causes a displacement of the object. In other words, a force causes the object's position to change. There are three components of work: force, displacement, and cause. A force must act on an object, the object must be displaced, and the force must cause the displacement.

THE ENGINEERING DESIGN PROCESS

The engineering design process is a series of steps that engineers use to solve a problem.

Define the Problem: What is the problem you are trying to solve?

Research: Gather information about the problem and other attempts to solve it.

Brainstorm: Use your imagination to think up as many ideas as possible to solve the problem.

Choose a Solution: Evaluate the ideas and pick the best one.

Prototype: Build or implement the solution.

Test: Test the solution you created to see if it performs as you expected. Gather feedback and make improvements as needed.

AN AMAZING FEAT

7

Archimedes (c. 287–c. 212 BCE) was an Ancient Greek scientist and inventor. Archimedes lived in the Greek colony of Sicily for much of his life and traveled to Alexandria, Egypt, to study. He was fascinated by how things worked. Archimedes identified three of the six simple machines—the lever, pulley, and screw—and demonstrated how each created a mechanical advantage. He is credited with saying, "Give me a lever long enough and a place to stand, and I will move the world." Archimedes's work led to several inventions, including a hydraulic screw that could raise water from a lower to a higher level. He is also credited with inventing the catapult, which the Greeks used to hurl heavy boulders at the Roman army.

● ● ● ● ● ● ● ●

Another way of saying this is that work is done when a force is used to move an object over a distance. Mathematically, work can be calculated as force times distance.

$$\text{Work (W)} = \text{Force (F)} \times \text{Distance (D)}$$

Work occurs all around us. For example, think about what happens when you pick up a backpack. As you lift it, the muscles in your arm exert a force on the backpack. The backpack changes position as you raise it to your shoulder. The force exerted by your arm causes the backpack to move. Your arm is doing work.

MAKING WORK EASIER

Simple machines make work easier. They change a force's direction, distance, or strength. For example, a pulley is a simple machine that makes work easier by changing the direction of a force. When you raise a flag on a flagpole, you pull down on a rope attached to a pulley to move the flag up.

Other simple machines change the distance of a force. Imagine you need to lift a heavy box full of books off the ground. You'll need to exert a lot of force to pick up and move the box of books.

FULL STEAM

There are simple machines in the human body! Arms, teeth, legs—even toes are simple machines that do work to make a body function.

Instead of lifting the heavy box, you could push it up an inclined plane. Pushing the box up the inclined plane is easier—but you'll have to move it a longer distance than if you had lifted it straight up.

ENGINEERING | INTRODUCTION

Some simple machines change the strength of a force. Have you ever tried to pry off a bottle cap with just your hands? No matter how hard you push and pull, the cap stays on tight. What if you tried using a bottle opener? A bottle opener is a type of simple machine called a lever. When you move the bottle opener's handle up, you apply a force to the handle. The bottle opener strengthens the force across its length and pops off the cap.

WORK INPUT = WORK OUTPUT

Simple machines make work easier but do not change the amount of work done. In physics, energy is the ability to do work. The amount of energy that is used to do the work is equal to the amount of work that gets done. The law of conservation of energy states that energy is not created or destroyed in a closed system—it is converted from one form to another form. For example, a car engine burns gasoline, which converts the chemical energy in gasoline into the mechanical energy to do the work of moving the car.

Every job requires a certain amount of work to complete—that amount does not change. Simple machines can change a force's direction, distance, or strength, but there will always be a tradeoff for these changes. If you use less force to move an object, you'll need to move it over a greater distance. If you move the object over a smaller distance, you must exert a greater force on it.

Simple machines provide a mechanical advantage. They make it easier to get work done. Often, work seems hard because it requires a lot of force. Using less force, even over a longer distance, can make the work easier.

VOCAB LAB

Write down what you think each word means. What root words can you find to help you? What does the context of the word tell you?

archaeologist, compound machine, displacement, force, inclined plane, law of conservation of energy, lever, mechanical advantage, pulley, screw, simple machine, wedge, wheel and axle, and **work**

Compare your definitions with those of your friends or classmates. Did you all come up with the same meanings? Turn to the text and glossary if you need help.

AN AMAZING FEAT

SIX SIMPLE MACHINES

There are six simple machines in engineering that we'll be investigating in this book.

Inclined plane: An inclined plane is a flat, sloped surface. Pushing a heavy object up an inclined plane is easier than lifting it. A ramp is an example of an inclined plane.

Lever: A lever is a flat board or arm with a pivot point called a fulcrum. When you push down on one end of a lever, the other end rises. The longer the board, the easier it is to lift a heavy object on the other end. A pair of scissors and a seesaw are examples of levers.

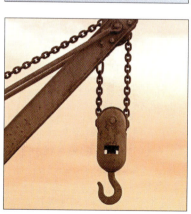

Pulley: A pulley is a wheel on a stationary axle. You pull a rope connected to the wheel to raise an object. A pulley is what raises the flag on a flagpole.

TEXT TO WORLD

What simple machines do you see around you right now? What are they used for?

ENGINEERING | INTRODUCTION

Screw: A screw is an inclined plane called a thread wrapped around a rod. When you turn a screw, it pulls two things together. The cap on a water bottle is an example of a screw.

Wedge: A wedge is wider at one end and tapers to a point. Wedges are used to split things, hold things, or push something apart. An axe is an example of a wedge.

Wheel and axle: A circular wheel is connected to a thin rod called an axle. When the wheel turns, the axle also turns. A wheel and axle lift and move loads. Cars use wheels and axles to move.

Mechanical, structural, civil, and many other types of engineering are based on the six simple machines that humans have been using for thousands of years. The inclined plane, lever, pulley, screw, wedge, and wheel and axle are used to build roads, skyscrapers, vehicles, engines, and even other tools. They are the building blocks from which all more complicated machines are built.

In this book, you'll discover the mechanics behind the six simple machines, along with their history, evolution, and potential future. Let's get to work with simple machines!

KEY QUESTIONS

- How did some ancient civilizations build towering structures without the benefit of modern machinery?

- What is the mathematical definition of work? How do simple machines change the amount of work a person needs to do?

AN AMAZING FEAT

Inquire & Investigate

WHERE ARE THE SIMPLE MACHINES?

Humans have been using simple machines for centuries. Simple machines make work easier. They create a mechanical advantage that reduces the force or effort needed to complete a job. You have probably used simple machines without even knowing it! In this activity, you'll investigate which simple machines you use at home.

- **Look around your house for small tools or gadgets that use one or more simple machines.** For example, you might find scissors, a corkscrew, can opener, garlic press, barbecue tongs, hand drill, wind-up toy, pencil sharpener, stapler, garage door opener, shovel, knife, wagon, wheelbarrow, and more.

- **For each tool or gadget you find, determine which simple machine it uses to work.** Is the tool a compound machine? If yes, what simple machines does it combine? You might need to do a little research about the six types of simple machines: inclined plane, lever, pulley, screw, wedge, and wheel and axle.

- **Create a data table with the information you collect.** How many of each type of simple machine did you find? What type of simple machine was most common in your home? What was the least common? Make a graph of your data.

- **Share your graph with your class.** How do your results compare with those of your classmates? What was the most common simple machine for the entire class? What was the least common simple machine?

> To investigate more, choose one of the tools you use at home. What do you use this tool to do? How does this tool help you? How would you accomplish the same task if you did not have this tool? Why does the tool make work easier? What is the tradeoff?

ENGINEERING | INTRODUCTION

Chapter 1
Inclined Planes

Where can you find inclined planes in daily life?

Many public buildings have accessible ramps—those are inclined planes! Check them out at skate parks, airports, playgrounds, roadways, and many more places.

● ● ● ● ● ● ● ●

An inclined plane is a simple machine that makes it easier to move heavy objects up or down. You might have seen and even used an inclined plane without realizing it. A ramp at a store, a slide at the playground, or a driveway that slopes up to a garage are all examples of inclined planes.

An inclined plane is one of the most straightforward simple machines. It is a flat surface that is tilted so one end is higher than the other. The inclined plane connects a higher place to a lower place. It does not move when it is used—an inclined plane remains still.

Inclined planes make it easier to move something from a lower place to a higher place and vice versa. Lifting an object straight up requires a lot of effort. Imagine lifting a dirt bike into a pickup truck. Pretty tough! Now, imagine a ramp from the ground to the truck bed. You can push the dirt bike up the ramp much more easily than you can lift it. And you can roll it back out to the ground without dropping it. That ramp is a type of inclined plane.

ENGINEERING | CHAPTER ONE

HOW DO INCLINED PLANES WORK?

The laws of physics tell us that lifting an object to a certain height requires a certain amount of work. You might think that studying for a math test is work, but that's not what scientists mean when they talk about work. In physics, work occurs when a force acts upon an object to cause it to move.

The laws of physics also tell us that the amount of work needed to move a particular object is always the same. We can, however, use a simple machine such as an inclined plane to change how the work is done.

Work has two components:
force
and distance.

As we saw earlier, force and distance have an inverse relationship when calculating work. When one increases, the other decreases.

Imagine you must climb a large hill. You have two choices: a staircase that goes directly to the top or a gently sloping path that winds around the hill. Both options will get you from the bottom of the hill to the top. Which one will you choose?

The stairs are the shortest way to the top. But the stairs take a lot of effort. You might be gasping for breath by the time you get to the top! On the other hand, the slope is a longer distance to walk. But your leg muscles won't be burning by the time you reach the hilltop.

SIEGE RAMPS

In 70 CE, a group of Jewish rebels retreated to the fortress of Masada, located high on a cliff overlooking the Dead Sea in modern-day Israel. The Roman army followed. To reach the fort without having to climb the cliff, the Romans built a massive earth ramp— an inclined plane—on the side of the fortress. The enormous ramp was 1,968 feet long and rose 200 feet to meet the fortress walls. Once the ramp was complete, the Roman army pushed a siege tower up the ramp to the fortress walls. The siege tower carried a battering ram that the Romans used to pound a hole in the fort's walls. Eventually, the Roman army was able to break through Masada's walls.

INCLINED PLANES

An ancient Roman aqueduct

In this example, the slope acts as an inclined plane. The amount of work you do to reach the hilltop is the same no matter which path you take. The slope makes the work of reaching the hilltop easier because you use less effort, or force, across a greater distance. The force needed to climb the hill is spread along the slope, making it feel easier. That is the magic of an inclined plane—although the work is the same, it feels easier!

Like all simple machines, Inclined planes provide a mechanical advantage. Mechanical advantage is the number of times a simple machine increases the force used to perform a task. For example, if you use a simple machine with a mechanical advantage of 2, you can lift an object weighing 40 pounds with an input force of only 20 pounds.

FULL STEAM

Roman emperors appointed a *curator aquarum*, or "water curator," to oversee the extensive maintenance of the aqueducts.

16   ENGINEERING | CHAPTER ONE

We calculate mechanical advantage by comparing the output force (the force put out by the machine) to the input force (the force you put into the machine). We measure force in newtons—named after Sir Isaac Newton (1643–1727), an English scientist famous for his scientific and mathematical discoveries. When measuring mechanical advantage, a mechanical advantage of 3 means that for every 1 newton of force you put into a simple machine, the machine produces 3 newtons of force.

Let's take a closer look at how mechanical advantage works for inclined planes. In this example, the inclined plane has a height (h) of 2 feet (ft) and a distance (D) of 5 ft. To calculate the mechanical advantage (MA) of this inclined plane, we use the following equation.

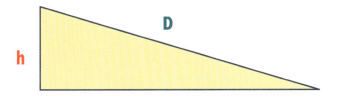

$$MA = D / h$$
$$MA = 5 \text{ ft} / 2 \text{ ft}$$
$$MA = 2.5$$

The mechanical advantage of this inclined plane is 2.5. That means for every newton of force used to push an object up the incline, the simple machine multiples it by a factor of 2.5.

Would you rather push a box up a steeper or more gradual slope? The gradual slope seems easier because you exert less force to push the box—it has a greater mechanical advantage.

ROMAN AQUEDUCTS

Between 312 BCE and 226 CE, Ancient Roman engineers constructed aqueducts to carry water to cities and towns. The aqueducts ran hundreds of miles across the Roman Empire and carried fresh water from lakes and springs through pipes, tunnels, bridges, and canals. The engineers who designed the aqueducts used gravity and inclined planes to move the fresh water to cities and towns for drinking, bathing, public fountains, and irrigation. In Rome, 11 aqueduct systems brought fresh water into the city from as far as 57 miles away. Today, some of the aqueducts still operate and provide Rome with water. For example, the Aqua Virgo aqueduct built around 19 BCE carries water to Rome's Trevi Fountain today. This is an instance where inclined planes were used to move material down instead of up!

INCLINED PLANES   17

Watch this video to learn how Galileo used inclined planes to study the motion of objects. What did he learn? **How did inclined planes make his observations possible?**

PBS Galileo inclined plane

Let's take a closer look at how this works. In this example, the inclined plane has the same height (h) of 2 ft that we saw in the previous example. However, the slope is more gradual and the distance (D) is longer at 8 ft.

What is the mechanical advantage of this inclined plane?

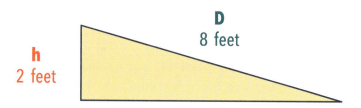

$$MA = D / h$$
$$MA = 8 \text{ ft} / 2 \text{ ft}$$
$$MA = 4$$

The mechanical advantage is 4. That means that for every newton of force used to push an object up the incline, the inclined plane multiples it by a factor of 4. This inclined plane has a greater mechanical advantage than the first inclined plane. Moving an object up the longer, more gradual slope requires less force. Which slope would you prefer to push your box up?

FULL STEAM

The inclined plane was the last of the six simple machines to be recognized as a simple machine.

18 ENGINEERING | CHAPTER ONE

FORCES ON AN INCLINED PLANE

Forces are around us all the time. Every object—including you!—is constantly pulled and pushed in different directions by forces. A force is a push or pull on an object when it interacts with another object. For example, when you sit on a chair, you exert a force on the chair and the chair exerts a force back on you.

A force is a vector, meaning it has both a magnitude (size) and direction. To describe a force, you need to describe its magnitude and direction. For example, when describing the force used to push a chair, you'd talk about both the size of the push and its direction. In a diagram, a force is often represented by an arrow. The arrow's length shows the force's magnitude, while the arrow points in the direction the force is acting.

What about the forces that affect an object that's simply sitting still?

Normal force and gravity affect a box sitting on a flat surface. Normal force (F_N) is a force that always acts perpendicular to the surface on which an object rests. When the box sits on a flat surface, gravity (F_W) pulls it toward Earth's center and exerts a force down on the surface. The surface exerts an equal and opposite normal force back on the box. The two forces on the object are balanced.

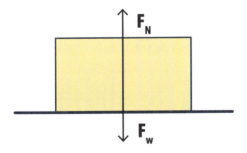

FRICTION

Friction is a force that opposes motion and acts in the opposite direction. No surface is 100 percent smooth. Even something that looks smooth to the naked eye might be rough or bumpy when looked at under a microscope. All those bumps, no matter how microscopic, grab onto the bumps of any object they contact. When they do, it creates friction. Rub your palms together. Feel the heat? That's evidence of friction between your hands! The amount of friction generated depends on the materials. A surface that is rougher or bumpier, such as gravel, creates more friction than a smoother surface, such as plastic. Heavier objects that press against a surface with greater force also create greater friction. This is another reason why pushing a heavy box across the floor is harder than pushing a lighter box.

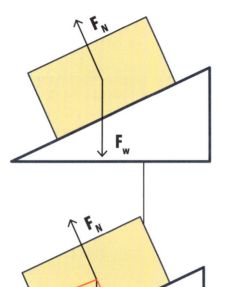

The net force is the sum of all the forces acting on an object. For the box on the flat surface, normal force and gravity are equal and opposite in direction. They cancel each other out, and the box does not move.

What happens to these forces when the box sits on an inclined plane? The normal force is always perpendicular to the surface. Because the inclined plane is sloped, the direction of the normal force changes and is perpendicular to the tilted surface. It no longer directly opposes the force of gravity. Normal force and gravity are now unbalanced.

The gravity force can be split into two components. One component is parallel to the surface (F_x). The second component is perpendicular (F_y) to the surface.

The diagram shows that the normal force (F_N) and the perpendicular component of gravity (F_y) are equal and opposite. These two forces cancel each other out. However, a force—the parallel component of gravity (F_x)—is still acting on the box. The net force on the box is equal to the parallel component of gravity (F_x). It causes the box to start to slide down the inclined plane.

But what affects how fast the box will slide down the inclined plane? Friction! Friction is the result of two surfaces rubbing together and is the third force that affects how fast the box slides down the inclined plane. Friction opposes motion and acts in the opposite direction. It slows the box's slide down the inclined plane. Friction also makes it harder to push the box up the inclined plane.

Watch this video to learn more about Roman aqueducts. **Why does it make sense to build aqueducts underground?**

Ancient Rome Live aqueduct

20 ENGINEERING | CHAPTER ONE

INCLINED PLANES IN HISTORY

Now that we've learned how an inclined plane works, how can we take advantage of inclined planes? Humans have been using inclined planes for thousands of years. Early humans likely first observed inclined planes in nature. A mountain is an example of a natural inclined plane. Early humans probably noticed that moving objects up mountains that were not as steep took less effort. Then, they adapted nature's inclined plane to create a simple machine they could use to help move heavy objects and build structures.

Archaeologists believe that humans began using inclined planes independently in several ancient civilizations. As we learned in the Introduction, the Ancient Egyptians built earth ramps, a type of inclined plane, to push heavy blocks so they could build the pyramids. Archaeologists have uncovered evidence that ancient people in Mesopotamia and China also built ramps to move construction materials when building large structures.

Inclined planes quickly became a crucial part of construction and transportation.

The Ancient Romans and Ancient Greeks used ramps to move materials during the construction of temples, amphitheaters, aqueducts, and other structures. They built roads and pathways that included inclined planes to make it easier to move goods and travel across different types of terrain.

ANCIENT ACCESSIBLE DESIGN

Did you know that ramps for the elderly or people who have trouble walking are not a modern invention? Archaeologists have uncovered evidence that the Ancient Greeks built stone ramps to help people who could not climb stairs get into holy sites more easily. Some of these ramps are more than 2,300 years old. They are some of the oldest known examples of architecture designed to be accessible.

● ● ● ● ● ● ● ●

INCLINED PLANES

As centuries passed, engineers developed new ways inclined planes could be used. They incorporated inclined planes into machinery, transportation systems, and countless everyday items. In factories, inclined planes on assembly lines moved materials smoothly throughout production. Loading ramps for trucks, ships, and planes made loading and unloading goods easier. In mining, inclined planes helped bring ore and other materials found deep underground to the surface.

Today, inclined planes are at work all around us. Accessible ramps help people in wheelchairs get somewhere without using stairs. A sloped driveway helps get a car from the road to a garage at a different level. A highway ramp connects a road to a bridge. Parking garages use ramps so cars can drive from one level to the next. A dump truck mechanically raises and lowers its truck bed to perform as an inclined plane. Some inclined planes are even meant for fun, such as water slides, ski slopes, and the bowls of a skateboard park.

The inclined plane is a useful simple machine that has become an essential tool of engineering.

TEXT TO WORLD

In what ways do inclined planes make your life easier? Do you use ramps? Stairs?

KEY QUESTIONS

- How does mechanical advantage help on construction sites?

- What ancient architecture might not exist without inclined planes?

22 ENGINEERING | CHAPTER ONE

FRICTION ON AN INCLINED PLANE

Inquire & Investigate

When you pull or push an object up an inclined plane, the force of friction opposes your motion. Friction pushes in the opposite direction of motion, making it harder to move the box up the inclined plane. In this activity, we'll investigate how different materials on a ramp can affect friction.

- **Build an inclined plane using materials you have on hand.** Let the quarter slide down the ramp and time how long it takes. Record your observation.

- **Examine the items with different textures.** Which do you think will create the most friction? Why? Which do you think will create the least amount of friction? Why?

- **Test the texture of each material by placing it on the inclined plane.** Hold the top of the material in place on the ramp.

- **Slide the quarter on its flat side down the ramp.** Use a stopwatch or timer to record how long the coin takes to reach the bottom of the ramp. Record your observations and results in your science notebook.

- **Repeat this with each textured material.** Record your observations and results.

- **What material produced the fastest slide?** What material produced the slowest slide? What does this tell you about the friction produced by each material? Compare your predictions to the actual results. Do they match?

Ideas for Supplies

- materials to build an inclined plane (ruler, board, books, etc.)
- a quarter
- timer
- items with different textures such as sandpaper, printer paper, plastic, fabric, felt, sandpaper
- science notebook

To investigate more, change the slope or length of the inclined plane to make it higher or longer. Repeat the experiment. How does changing the inclined plane affect friction?

INCLINED PLANES

Inquire & Investigate

Ideas for Supplies

- table
- several books
- rubber band
- scissors
- paper clip
- ruler
- tape
- rice
- plastic sandwich bag with twist tie
- 12-inch piece of string
- science notebook
- two boards, pieces of cardboard, or other flat materials of different lengths

> To investigate more, vary the height of the book stack to change the slope of the inclined plane. How does changing the slope affect the force needed to move the bag of rice?

INVESTIGATING FORCE ON AN INCLINED PLANE

An inclined plane is a simple machine that reduces the amount of force needed to move an object to a specific height. The inclined plane spreads that force across a longer distance. As a result, you need less force to move the object. In this activity, you'll test how the slope and length of an inclined plane affect force.

- **Stack two books on a table.**

- **Use a rubber band, paper clip, ruler, and tape to make a simple device to measure force.** Cut the rubber band so that it is one long piece of stretchy rubber. Tie the paper clip to one end of the rubber band. Hang the paper clip end of the rubber band over the top of the ruler until the bottom of the paper clip reaches the 3.5-inch mark on the ruler. Tape the other part of the rubber band to the back of the ruler.

- **Place a handful of rice in the plastic bag.** Seal it with the twist tie.

- **Tie one end of the string to the plastic bag.** Tie the other end of the string to the paper clip.

- **Hold the ruler vertically next to the stack of books.** Lift straight up until the bottom of the bag hangs at the same level as the top of the book stack.

ENGINEERING | CHAPTER ONE

Inquire & Investigate

- **The rubber band will stretch from the force needed to raise the rice bag.**
  - How far does the rubber band stretch? In your science notebook, record where the bottom of the paper clip reaches on the ruler.
  - How does the force needed to raise the rice bag change if you use an inclined plane?

- **Using the shorter board, create an inclined plane.** Rest one end of the board at the top of the book stack and the other end on the table.

- **Hold the ruler and pull the bag up the inclined plane to the top of the book stack.** Where does the end of the paper clip stretch to on the ruler? Record the number.

- **Repeat the experiment using the longer board as an inclined plane.** Record your measurements.

- **The stretch of the rubber band, as measured on the ruler, represents the force needed to lift the bag of rice to a specific height.**
  - Did it take more effort to lift the bag straight up or pull it up the ramp?
  - What happened when you made a longer ramp?
  - How did increasing the distance affect the force needed to move the bag of rice?
  - How do your results explain how an inclined plane makes it easier to lift a load?

VOCAB LAB

Write down what you think each word means. What root words can you find to help you? What does the context of the word tell you?

aqueduct, friction, gravity, input force, inverse, magnitude, net force, newton, normal force, output force, perpendicular, siege, and **vector**

Compare your definitions with those of your friends or classmates. Did you all come up with the same meanings? Turn to the text and glossary if you need help.

INCLINED PLANES   25

Inquire & Investigate

Ideas for Supplies

- construction paper
- plastic straws
- paper towel rolls
- jumbo craft sticks
- heavy-duty aluminum foil
- heavy cardstock or cereal boxes
- masking tape or duct tape
- string
- scissors
- several ping-pong balls

To investigate more, try using a different ball, such as a golf ball or whiffle ball. How does a different ball affect the function of the aqueduct?

BUILD A MINIATURE AQUEDUCT

The Ancient Romans used gravity and inclined planes to create a system of aqueducts to provide water to populated areas. Now it's your turn! In this activity, you'll design a miniature aqueduct system to transport a ping-pong ball using inclined planes and gravity.

- **Using the available materials, design, plan, and build a mini aqueduct.** Follow the engineering design process:

  1. Define the problem
  2. Research solutions
  3. Brainstorm ideas
  4. Plan the design
  5. Build a prototype
  6. Test the prototype and make improvements to your design

- **How effective was your design at moving the ping-pong ball?**

  - What, if any, improvements did you make to the design after testing it?

  - What challenges did you encounter during the design process?

  - How did you use inclined planes and gravity to keep the ping-pong ball moving?

Chapter 2
Levers

How do levers reduce the amount of force needed to do work?

Need to get a nail out of your wall? Design a marshmallow catapult? Stand on your toes? All of these actions use levers!

● ● ● ● ● ● ● ●

Have you ever ridden a seesaw at the neighborhood park? If you have, you've experienced a lever at work. A lever is a long bar or rod that rotates around a fixed point called a fulcrum. A lever is one of the six simple machines that make it easier to do work. We use levers to help us move or lift things with less effort.

Imagine if you needed to lift your older brother. He weighs more than you, so lifting him would be challenging, if not impossible. But if he's sitting on the other side of a seesaw, you can push down on your side of the seesaw and your brother rises into the air. It's so much easier than trying to lift him in your arms! A seesaw is a lever in action.

Let's look at levers, how they work, and why they are so important in engineering!

28 | ENGINEERING | CHAPTER TWO

HOW LEVERS WORK

Levers use torque to move or lift objects. Torque is a force that causes an object to rotate around a pivot point. Every lever has a fulcrum, which is the lever's pivot point. When you apply a force to one part of the lever by pushing or pulling it, the lever swings about the fulcrum and produces an action at the other end of the lever.

The force you apply to the lever is called the effort. The side of the lever that moves up and raises a heavy weight is called the load.

Where is the fulcrum on a seesaw? In the middle! Both sides of the seesaw are the same distance from the fulcrum. In other examples, however, the fulcrum is closer to one end of the lever, and the lever's sides are different lengths. If you use a long stick to pry a large rock out of the ground, the fulcrum will probably be closer to the rock than to your hands.

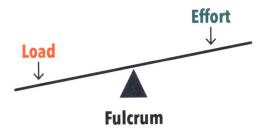

The location of the fulcrum on a lever affects how much effort you need to move an object. The farther away from the fulcrum you apply the effort, the less effort you need to move the load. So, the longer the lever arm, the easier it is to move a heavy object.

As with inclined planes, levers have tradeoffs. When you reduce the effort needed to lift a heavy load, the distance increases. You must move the lever a greater distance to lift the load. We can see this relationship in this equation.

Effort × Effort Arm = Load × Load Arm

- Effort arm = the distance from the effort to the fulcrum
- Load arm = the distance from the load to the fulcrum

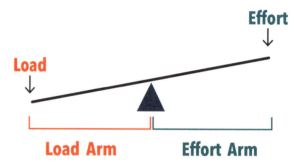

For example, let's look at a lever that is 10 feet long with a 50-pound load, such as a heavy box of books. When the lever's fulcrum is exactly in the middle, the lever arm and the effort arm are both 5 feet long.

Effort × 5 ft = 50 lbs × 5 ft
Effort × 5 ft = 250 lbs × ft
Effort = 250 lbs × ft / 5 ft
Effort = 50 lbs

A BALANCE SCALE

The simple balance scale is an example of a first-class lever in action. It has a central pivot point (fulcrum) in the middle of two arms of equal length. To use the scale, you place an object of unknown weight on one side of the scale (load). You then add known weights to the other side of the scale (effort), which moves one side of the scale up or down. The scale is balanced and level when the force on one side is equal to the load on the other side. And now you know how much your object weighs!

● ● ● ● ● ● ● ●

ENGINEERING | CHAPTER TWO

In this example, the effort and load are equal. You need to apply 50 pounds of force to move a load of 50 pounds. However, a lever makes your work easier by changing the direction of the force you apply. It feels like less work to push down on the end of the lever to move the load up than it does to lift the load—the 50-pound box of books—in your arms.

FULL STEAM

The word "lever" comes from the French word *elever* which means "to raise."

Now, let's look at what happens when you move the fulcrum closer to the load. This time, the lever arm is 8 feet long and the load arm is 2 feet long.

$$\text{Effort} \times 8 \text{ ft} = 50 \text{ lbs} \times 2 \text{ ft}$$
$$\text{Effort} \times 8 \text{ ft} = 100 \text{ lbs} \times \text{ft}$$
$$\text{Effort} = 100 \text{ lbs} \times \text{ft} / 8 \text{ ft}$$
$$\text{Effort} = 12.5 \text{ lbs}$$

This time, you need to apply only 12.5 pounds of force to lift the 50-pound load. The longer effort arm lets you use less force to move the load. The tradeoff is that you must move the lever arm a greater distance.

LEVERS AND MECHANICAL ADVANTAGE

A lever provides mechanical advantage and, therefore, makes work easier by changing the direction or strength of an applied force. As we saw earlier, the locations of the fulcrum, effort, and load on the lever affect mechanical advantage.

FRICTION AND LEVERS

As with all simple machines, levers provide mechanical advantage to make a task easier by increasing force. Optimal mechanical advantage is without friction. However, all simple machines must overcome friction in the real world. In levers, the force of friction at the fulcrum can reduce their mechanical advantage. Even with reduced mechanical advantage, levers are still a highly effective simple machine that can make work easier.

• • • • • • • •

The longer the lever arm, the easier it is to move the load because the lever provides a greater mechanical advantage. You can calculate a lever's mechanical advantage (MA) using this formula.

MA = Effort Arm / Load Arm

An increase in a lever's effort arm increases the lever's mechanical advantage because less force is needed to lift the load. At the same time, the lever's effort arm moves a greater distance. In this way, a lever trades less force for greater distance.

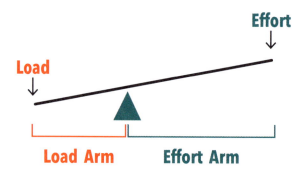

FIRST-CLASS LEVERS

Levers are divided into three main classes based on the location of the effort, load, and fulcrum. A first-class lever has a fulcrum between the force (effort) and the load (object you're trying to move). First-class levers are great for lifting heavy loads with less effort. They can change the direction and strength of an applied force.

A seesaw is an example of a first-class lever. The fulcrum is in the middle. When you push down one end (effort), the load is raised at the other end. The lever changes the direction of the applied force.

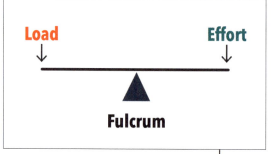

First-Class Lever

ENGINEERING | CHAPTER TWO

Scissors are another example of a first-class lever. The fulcrum is the point where the two blades meet. When you press the handles together (effort), perhaps to cut some paper, the blades cut through the paper (load). Scissors are actually a compound machine—they have more than one simple machine. The sharp blade is a wedge. You'll learn more about compound machines in Chapter 7.

You can also use a claw hammer as a first-class lever to pull a nail from a wall. Without the hammer, you could try to pull the nail with your fingers—ouch! The force needed to move the nail, even a small distance, is often more than you can generate with only your hand. With a claw hammer, you use the claw to grip the nail (load) and move the hammer handle to pry the nail from the wall. The hammer's head acts as a fulcrum as it rests on the wall. The hammer's handle is the lever, and you apply effort where you grip the handle. The claw hammer trades force for distance. The closer the hammer's fulcrum is to the nail (load), the farther you must move the handle to pull the nail from the wall.

SECOND-CLASS LEVERS

In a second-class lever, the load is between the fulcrum and the effort, and the load is always closer to the fulcrum than to the effort. The closer the load is to the fulcrum, the less effort is needed to move it. Second-class levers allow you to use less effort to create a larger output force and move the load. They change a force's strength to make work easier.

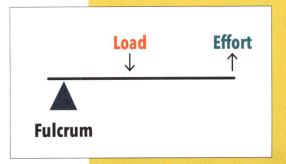

Second-Class Lever

LEVERS 33

This dog is trying out a second-class lever!

A wheelbarrow is an example of a second-class lever. The wheel is the fulcrum, the load is what is in the wheelbarrow, and the effort is the force you apply to hold and pick up the handles to move the wheelbarrow. A second-class lever is often used to lift heavy objects because it provides a large mechanical advantage.

A wheel and its axle are another simple machine that you'll learn about in Chapter 6.

Paddles and crowbars are both examples of second-class levers.

FULL STEAM

A bottle opener is a second-class lever. The end that rests on the bottle cap (load) is the fulcrum. You pull up on the other end of the opener (effort) to pop the cap off the bottle.

ENGINEERING | CHAPTER TWO

THIRD-CLASS LEVERS

With a third-class lever, the effort is located between the load and the fulcrum, and the effort is always closer to the fulcrum than the load. A shovel is an example of a third-class lever. When you hold a shovel with two hands, the handle at the top is the fulcrum, where the lever pivots. Your other hand grips the middle of the lever and applies effort. The load is at the bottom of the lever and is the material you shovel.

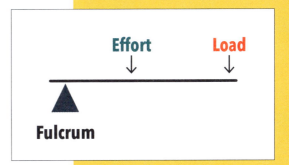

Third-Class Lever

A third-class lever can help you move something quickly or with precision. It is not the best choice for lifting something heavy because it actually requires more force to move the load than the weight of the load. Third-class levers are good for moving objects far distances, but they do require more force.

A broom is a third-class lever. When you sweep the floor with a broom, your top hand grips the broom handle and acts as the fulcrum. Your lower hand applies the effort and moves the broom back and forth. The broom bristles that sweep the dirt on the floor are the load (output). The broom's bristles move faster and over a greater distance than your hand as it applies the effort. The broom moves quickly over the floor. It does the work of sweeping faster than you could with only your hands.

LEVERS IN HISTORY

If you lived in the days of early civilization and you needed to dig a rock out of the dirt where you wanted to lay down, what would you use for a tool? Maybe a sturdy stick would help? That's a lever!

You can find levers inside musical instruments, including pianos, trumpets, and guitars. Even made-up instruments have levers. Take a look at this musical marble machine and spot the levers! **What other simple machines can you find?**

Wintergatan Marble Machine

LEVERS 35

Throughout history, levers have been essential in many inventions and advancements. This simple tool has enabled people to build, lift, and move objects that would otherwise have been impossible. As early as 5000 BCE, people used a lever in a simple balance scale. Larger levers were used to lift heavy materials for building.

During the Roman Empire, engineers invented siege weapons that used levers. One such weapon was a catapult called an onager. The onager used a large lever system to launch heavy objects such as stones, fire, or even burning tar at an enemy. The onager let soldiers launch objects much farther than they could have with human strength alone.

Simple machines are part of the art world, too. Take a look at this news piece about the sculptures of Dutch artist Theo Jansen. **What simple machines do you see at work?**

Theo Jansen New Yorker video

Siege weapons such as the onager helped the Roman army attack and overcome enemy fortresses and walls.

During the Industrial Revolution in the eighteenth and nineteenth centuries, levers became essential parts of many machines and tools. For example, power looms in textile mills used a precise system of levers, gears, and springs to weave fabric. Levers helped lift and move heavy materials and apply force exactly. With a lever, workers needed to apply only a small force to move large objects, which improved efficiency and reduced manual labor.

FULL STEAM

Sheet metal breaks use levers to bend sheet metal into new shapes.

Levers and machines allowed many production tasks to be automated, making mass manufacturing possible.

36 ENGINEERING | CHAPTER TWO

LEVERS IN ACTION

Today, levers are at work all around us. Levers are essential to many tools we use every day. They help us open containers, remove nails, move heavy loads, and pry apart objects. Levers in wheelbarrows, plows, and hoes make farming and gardening tasks easier.

In construction, levers help with building, demolition, and other tasks. The crowbar is an example of a common tool used in construction. The crowbar's long arm enables workers to lift or pry objects (load) by applying force at one end (effort). The crowbar's fulcrum multiplies the effort so the worker can move a heavy object more easily.

We use levers in sports, too. Levers are essential to the design of a lot of sports and exercise equipment. How far can you throw a baseball? Probably not as far as when you hit it with a baseball bat! The bat provides a mechanical advantage. Your arm applies a force to make the bat swing and the ball, which is the load, might just go flying across the ballpark. Swing a golf club and, again, you're using a lever.

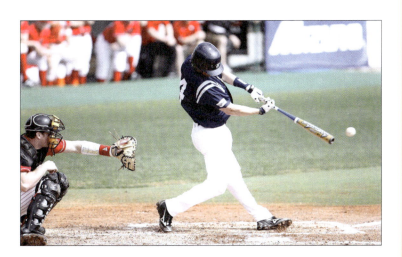

LIFTING WATER WITH A SHADUF

As far back as 3000 BCE, people used a long wooden lever called a shaduf to lift water. A shaduf was a long pole mounted between two vertical poles. On one end of the pole was a bucket attached with a rope. On the pole's other end was a heavy stone or piece of clay or other type of counterweight to balance the pole and help raise the bucket of water. To use the shaduf, a worker lowered the pole into a river or well to fill the bucket with water. Then, the worker pushed down on the other end of the pole to lift the bucket, with help from the counterweight. The worker moved the bucket of water to where it was needed. The shaduf was a simple tool commonly used in ancient times to water crops.

● ● ● ● ● ● ● ● ●

LEVERS

Watch this video to see people using shadufs in the 1940s. **How is modern farming different and what does that mean for farmers' daily lives?**

Pathe shaduf

TEXT TO WORLD

Look around your kitchen. What levers do you see there? What classes can you find?

Levers are an essential part of many complex machines. Robots in manufacturing and medicine use levers for precise movement. Spacecraft use levers to deploy landing gear, move robotic arms, and control different functions in space. Heavy machinery, such as construction cranes and excavators, combines levers with other simple machines to do the job. In many cars, the braking system uses levers and hydraulics to stop the vehicle.

LEVERS AND THE HUMAN BODY

Did you know your body has levers? Your muscles, bones, and joints form levers that allow you to move and perform all sorts of activities. In the human body, bones act as levers, while the joints serve as the fulcrums around which the bones pivot. Your skeletal muscles are attached to the bones. When the muscles contract, they create a force that causes the bones to move. Your body—or an object you want to hold or lift—is the load.

Your body uses all three classes of levers.

Your head is an example of a first-class lever. The spine is the fulcrum, while the neck muscles are the force or effort. The neck muscles move the front of your head, the load.

When you stand on the ball of your foot, you are using a second-class lever. The ball of the foot serves as the fulcrum, and your body's weight is the load. When your calf muscles contract, they create a lifting force that allows you to raise up your body.

In the human body, third-class levers are the most common. Your arm is an example of a third-class lever system. When you want to lift a heavy object or load, your elbow serves as a fulcrum.

ENGINEERING | CHAPTER TWO

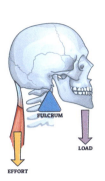
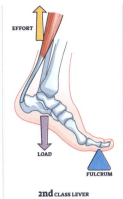
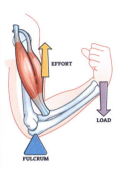

1st CLASS LEVER   2nd CLASS LEVER   3rd CLASS LEVER

Your bicep muscles exert force onto the lower arm, which causes rotation around the elbow joint and allows you to lift the object. What happens when you chew your morning cereal? Your jaw is another third-class lever at work.

Many activities involve different levers acting simultaneously in the human body. For example, when you walk, the levers in your toes, ankles, knees, and hips work together to move smoothly. Each lever must perform its function while allowing the others to perform their functions.

Levers are simple machines that help us move heavy things, lift objects, or change the direction of a force.

Whether you are riding a seesaw, prying up a rock with a crowbar, using a broom, swinging a baseball bat, or walking, you're using a lever. By understanding levers and how they work, you can see how they are part of many everyday objects and machines around us.

KEY QUESTIONS

- What levers might be at work at an Olympic Games?
- How does friction act on a lever serving as a fishing pole?

VOCAB LAB

Write down what you think each word means. What root words can you find to help you? What does the context of the word tell you?

applied force, counterweight, effort, Industrial Revolution, load, onager, pivot, and **torque**

Compare your definitions with those of your friends or classmates. Did you all come up with the same meanings? Turn to the text and glossary if you need help.

LEVERS

Inquire & Investigate

Ideas for Supplies

- science notebook
- string
- scissors
- duct tape
- wooden dowel or stick, approximately 12 inches long
- small paper cup
- small rock
- craft stick
- 2 large plastic cups
- 2 bowls
- water

To investigate more, adjust the placement of the dowel on the craft stick. How does changing the location of the pivot point (fulcrum) affect how the shaduf works?

BUILD A SHADUF TO LIFT WATER

Ancient farmers used a long wooden lever called a shaduf to lift water from rivers to irrigate crops and for other uses. This simple tool was incredibly effective at making it easier to move water. In this activity, you'll harness the power of a lever as you design and build a working model of a simple shaduf.

- **Cut a piece of string about 8 inches long.** Use duct tape to attach the string to one end of the wooden dowel or stick. Use duct tape to attach the other end of the string to the small paper cup.

- **Tape the small rock to the other end of the wooden dowel.**

- **To create a pivot point, place the craft stick horizontally across the bottoms of the two larger plastic cups.** Tape the ends of the stick securely to each cup to create a bridge-like structure.

- **Place the wooden dowel across the top of the craft stick.** When you move the dowel up and down, the rock should almost touch the table surface. Use string to secure the dowel to the craft stick.

- **Fill one bowl with water and leave the other empty.** Place your shaduf between the two bowls.

- **Test your shaduf and move water from one bowl to the other.** Does your design work as you thought it would? What adjustments, if any, would you make to improve your model?

40 ENGINEERING | CHAPTER TWO

BUILD A SIMPLE LEVER

Inquire & Investigate

Levers are used to lift and move heavy objects. In this activity, you'll build a model and test it.

- **Build a lever using the wooden ruler as the lever's arm.** Tape the bar of soap to one end of the lever. This will be the load the lever will lift.

- **Tape the cup to the other end of the ruler.** This is where you will apply effort to the lever.

- **Tape the bottle to a tabletop or other flat surface.** The bottle will be the fulcrum of the lever.

- **Position the ruler on the bottle (fulcrum) so the fulcrum is directly in the middle of the ruler.** The effort arm and load arm will be the same length.

- **Add marbles or pennies one at a time to the cup until the soap (load) lifts off the table.** In your science notebook, record the lengths of the effort arm and load arm and the number of marbles it took to lift the load off the table.

- **Increase the length of the effort arm by 1 inch.** How many marbles does it take to lift the load off the table? Record your data.

- **Continue increasing the effort arm length an inch at a time and repeat the experiment until you have multiple measurements.** Record your data each time.

- **Create a data table with your findings.** What pattern, if any, do you notice in the data? What is the relationship between the length of the effort arm and the effort (number of marbles) needed to lift the load?

Ideas for Supplies

- wooden ruler
- small bar of soap or something of similar weight
- masking tape
- small paper or plastic cup
- empty plastic soda or water bottle
- pennies, marbles, or other small, weighted objects
- science notebook

To investigate more, consider how you can change the lever you made in this activity to make it a second-class lever. How could you adapt this activity to test a second-class lever?

LEVERS 41

Inquire & Investigate

Ideas for Supplies

- craft sticks
- masking tape
- three 12-inch wooden skewers
- bendable plastic straw
- scissors
- dowels
- rubber band
- small plastic or paper cup
- cotton balls or other small projectiles

> To investigate more, see what happens if you move the cup on the catapult arm. Does the projectile travel less far or farther? Explain your results.

DESIGN AND BUILD A CATAPULT

A catapult is an example of a third-class lever. This type of lever has the load at one end, the fulcrum at the other end, and the effort applied in the middle. In this activity, you will build a model pyramid catapult and explore how it uses a lever to launch projectiles.

- **Use three craft sticks and masking tape to form a triangle.** Repeat this twice so that you have three identical triangles.

- **Place one triangle flat on a surface.** Place the other two triangles in a vertical direction to form a pyramid shape. Tape the triangles to each other to hold the pyramid shape.

- **To make the catapult arm, place three wooden skewers flat next to each other.** Tape them together near each end. Tape a craft stick to the middle of the skewers to reinforce the arm.

- **Cut a piece of straw and slide it about one inch over one end of the wooden skewers.** Tape the straw to the skewers so that it does not slide off.

- **Bend the straw perpendicular to the wooden skewers.** Insert the straw end into the catapult's pyramid base and tape the bent end to the pyramid frame. The bent straw creates a hinge for the catapult arm.

- **Loop the rubber band around the catapult arm.** Weave it under and over the catapult frame and back over the catapult arm.

ENGINEERING | CHAPTER TWO

Inquire & Investigate

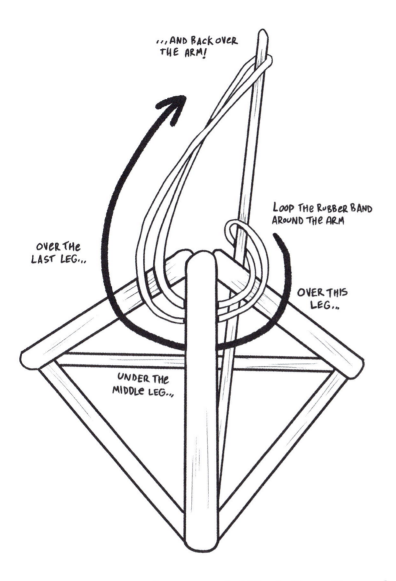

- **Tape the cup about one-half inch from the end of the catapult arm.**
- **To test the catapult, load a projectile into the cup.** Hold the front of the pyramid base with one hand and pull down the catapult arm with your other hand. Let go and see how far your projectile goes!

LEVERS

Chapter 3
Pulleys

What kinds of jobs do pulleys make easier?

Pulleys make it easier to lift heavy objects by changing the direction and amount of the force. You can find pulleys on construction sites, in office buildings, on flag poles, and in many other places.

● ● ● ● ● ● ● ● ●

If you need to get to the 10th floor of a building, would you rather take the stairs or the elevator? You could huff and puff up the stairs, but the elevator would be much less work. An elevator makes it easier by using a pulley, a simple machine.

A pulley is a simple machine used to lift and move heavy loads. Every pulley starts with a wheel. A rope or cable winds around the wheel's edge. Often, the wheel has a groove around its edge to hold the rope in place. The rope can be made of various materials, such as metal or nylon. One end of the rope is attached to an object (load). A person or a motor (force) pulls the other end of the rope, which causes the wheel to turn and raise the load.

A single pulley changes the direction of an applied force, making it easier to lift a load. Several pulleys used together—in a pulley system—can increase the strength of the applied force. A pulley system provides a powerful mechanical advantage to lift heavy objects with less effort.

FIXED VS. MOVEABLE PULLEYS

Pulleys can be fixed or moveable. As its name suggests, a fixed pulley is mounted on something and does not move. A fixed pulley primarily changes the direction of an applied force. When you pull on the pulley's rope, the pulley lifts an object.

A flagpole is an example of a fixed pulley. The flag is attached to a cord. When you pull one end of the cord, the flag goes up. To get the flag down, you pull the other end of the cord.

A fixed pulley does not reduce the amount of force needed to raise the flag but lets you apply force more comfortably and easily, pulling down instead of lifting.

A fixed pulley is helpful in raising an object to a height above your head. A counterweight at the end of the rope can also help reduce the force needed to raise the object. Gravity pulls on the counterweight, meaning you have to apply less force.

Have you ever seen a well with a bucket on a rope at the top? The bucket is lowered into the well and tugged back up with a fixed pulley.

A moveable pulley moves along a rope or cable. One end of the rope is attached to a fixed surface, while the other end is left free or attached to another fixed point. The load is attached to the moveable pulley. When you pull the rope, the pulley moves and lifts the load.

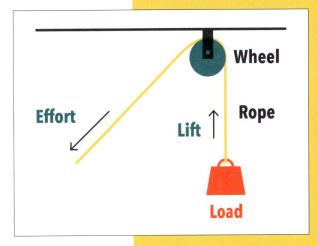

Fixed pulley

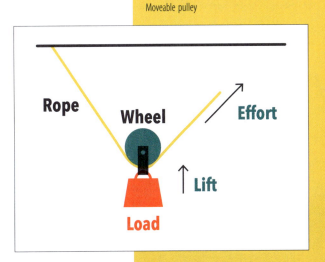

Moveable pulley

PULLEYS 47

COUNTERWEIGHTS

Cranes and other machines that use pulleys to lift heavy objects typically rely on counterweights. A counterweight balances the weight of the load and can help prevent the machine from tipping over as it lifts the load. The machine's motor does not need to apply force to support the load because the counterweight does that job. Instead, the motor only has to apply the force necessary to move the load.

• • • • • • • • •

Pulleys are used for lots of different activities. Watch this video for some examples. **Where do you encounter pulleys in your daily life?**

NatGen pulleys

A zipline is an example of a moveable pulley. The pulley is attached to the rider (the load). As the cable is pulled, the pulley and rider move along the zipline to its end.

You can find lots of moveable pulleys on sailboats. The sail lines move through fixed pulleys as sailors raise and lower the sails. Moveable pulleys make work easier by changing the strength of the applied force.

MECHANICAL ADVANTAGE OF PULLEYS

As with all simple machines, a pulley provides a mechanical advantage that makes work easier. The mechanical advantage depends on the number and type of pulleys being used. An easy way to determine a pulley system's mechanical advantage is to count the rope segments that lift the load. The more rope segments doing the lifting, the less force is needed.

In a single fixed pulley, only one rope segment lifts the load. In this system, the pulley does not increase the applied force. The mechanical advantage simply changes the direction of the applied force. It still feels easier to do the work because when you pull down on the rope, you can use your weight to help you.

Object 10 lbs

Force 10 lbs

48 ENGINEERING | CHAPTER THREE

A single moveable pulley has two rope segments to lift the load. In this system, the pulley does not change the direction of the force, but the mechanical advantage increases the force applied to the rope so you can use less effort to lift the load.

COMPOUND PULLEY SYSTEMS

If one pulley can make work easier, what about two pulleys? A compound pulley system combines a fixed and moveable pulley. In a compound pulley system, you still have two rope segments lifting the load, but, now, a third segment changes the direction of the applied force.

The mechanical advantage of the system remains 2, but it changes the direction of the applied force.

Using pulleys reduces the force needed to lift a heavy object.

The tradeoff, however, is distance. The length of rope needed to raise the object to the same height increases.

FULL STEAM

Tangle-web spiders use a pulley-like system made from silk threads to raise prey off the ground.

PULLEYS 49

Astronauts use simple machines, including pulleys, on the International Space Station. Watch this video to learn more. **How do some simple machines work differently in space?**

STEMonstrations: Simple Machines

MORE PULLEYS, MORE FORCE

The mechanical advantage of a pulley system is directly related to the number of moveable pulleys and the ropes that support the load.

The more ropes supporting the load in the pulley system, the greater the mechanical advantage.

A greater mechanical advantage allows you to lift heavier objects with less force. What do you think the tradeoff might be?

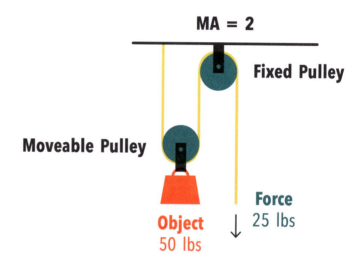

Imagine a worker must lift a 50-pound block. The block hangs 10 feet down from a single fixed pulley. To raise the block, the worker uses 50 pounds of force to pull the rope down 10 feet.

What if we added a moveable pulley to the system?

One moveable pulley carries the 50-pound load this time, and two rope segments support it. The block's weight is split equally between the two ropes. Each supports 25 pounds. The mechanical advantage of this system is 2.

FULL STEAM

A ski lift uses pulleys to move skiers to the top of the mountain.

50 ENGINEERING | CHAPTER THREE

To raise the block, the worker must apply a force of only 25 pounds. The point where the rope is fastened exerts the other 25 pounds of force on the rope. But to lift the block 10 feet, the worker must pull twice as much rope.

In this example, the worker must pull 20 feet of rope. That's the tradeoff between force and distance in a pulley system. When force decreases, the distance the rope moves increases.

What happens if we add even more pulleys to the system?

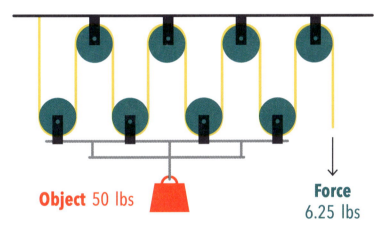

Object 50 lbs

Force 6.25 lbs

This pulley system has four moveable pulleys. Eight rope segments support the moveable pulleys. The mechanical advantage of this pulley system is 8. The worker needs to exert only 6.25 pounds of force to lift the 50-pound block but must pull the rope a longer distance—80 feet—to lift the block to the same height of 10 feet.

PULLEYS IN HISTORY

People have been using pulleys for thousands of years. Pulleys have been essential tools in construction, engineering, and everyday life.

DUMBWAITERS

In many nineteenth-century buildings, mechanical dumbwaiters delivered and carried various items from floor to floor. Dumbwaiters used a system of pulleys and weights to raise and lower a container in a shaft. They were popular in restaurants and wealthy homes, where the kitchens and dining rooms were often on different floors. The dining staff could shout down to the kitchen staff what they needed. The kitchen staff gathered the items, put them in the dumbwaiter, and pulled the rope to lift it and deliver its contents. Dumbwaiters were also popular in high-rise apartment buildings to help people move laundry, groceries, and other items from floor to floor. Eventually, electric motors were added—these are still in use today!

PULLEYS 51

The Eiffel Tower uses giant pulleys to operate its lift system.

Pulleys are thought to have been used in Mesopotamia since 2000 BCE. Farmers used water from the Rivers Tigris and Euphrates to grow crops—archaeologists believe pulleys were used to make this easier.

Archaeologists also believe that the Ancient Egyptians used pulley systems to help lift and move the massive stones used to build the pyramids. By changing the direction of the applied force with a single pulley, more workers could grab onto the rope and pull.

When more workers pulled the rope, less effort was needed from each individual. The Egyptians likely designed a system of ramps, pulleys, and levers to maneuver each heavy block into place.

FULL STEAM

Leonardo da Vinci designed a robotic knight that was meant to move with a series of pulleys.

ENGINEERING | CHAPTER THREE

The Ancient Romans used pulleys in civil engineering to help them build massive structures such as aqueducts, temples, amphitheaters, and roads.

Pulleys made it possible to lift and move heavy stones and other building materials for structures such as the Colosseum. Roman workers used pulleys to raise large stones to build walls and roofs on buildings. Human workers or animals powered the pulley systems by pulling on the pulleys' ropes.

The Ancient Greek scientist Archimedes studied pulleys and how they worked. He is credited with creating the block-and-tackle pulley system, which uses multiple pulleys to increase mechanical advantage. Archimedes is also said to have used his compound system of pulleys to lift large ships out of the water.

With time, more complex pulley systems emerged, such as those used in cranes and other heavy machinery. In France, construction on the iconic Eiffel Tower relied on pulleys and cranes. Workers used pulleys and cranes to lift the structure's heavy iron beams and other materials into place to build the tower. These simple machines allowed workers to finish the tower in March 1889, only 22 months after they started.

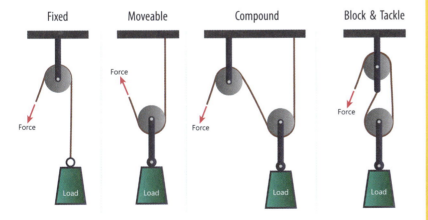

ELEVATORS

An elevator is a modern machine that uses pulleys and counterweights in its design. An elevator is an example of a single-pulley system. The elevator car is attached to a cable that runs over a pulley fixed at the top of the elevator shaft. A counterweight at the other end of the cable balances the weight of the elevator car and its passengers. The counterweight is pulled by gravity to help raise the elevator car. A motor moves the cable through the pulley system to raise and lower the elevator car. The motor needs only enough force to raise the difference in the weight of the car with its passengers and the counterweight. Without the pulley and counterweight, the elevator's motor would have to be much larger to handle the combined weight of the car and its passengers.

BLOCK-AND-TACKLE PULLEY SYSTEM

One type of compound pulley system is a block-and-tackle system. A simple block-and-tackle pulley system combines two fixed pulleys and two moveable pulleys with one rope wound around the pulleys. When you pull the rope, the weight of the load is spread across the four rope segments, which means the force you apply to lift the load is multiplied by 4. A block-and-tackle pulley system can have many pulleys. The more pulleys, the greater the force and the greater mechanical advantage provided by the pulleys. Block-and-tackle systems are used on drilling rigs and to move heavy stage equipment in theaters.

The Panama Canal is one of the world's greatest engineering marvels. Completed in 1914, the canal stretches 40 miles across the Isthmus of Panama to connect the Atlantic and Pacific Oceans.

Pulleys and cranes were an essential part of the canal's construction. Workers used these tools to move heavy materials as they dug the canal and built its system of locks.

PULLEYS IN ACTION

Today, pulleys help us in many ways. Pulleys make it much easier to lift and move things. At home, you use pulleys whenever you pull up a window blind, raise and lower the laundry on a pulley clothesline, or open a garage door. A water well

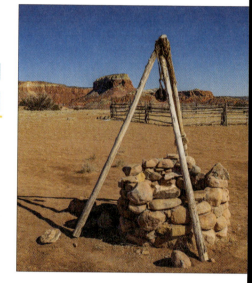

with a rope and bucket uses a simple fixed-pulley system to raise and lower the bucket of water.

In the gym, you can find pulley systems on exercise equipment. A weight machine uses a pulley system that allows you to lift weights with less force and target different muscle groups more effectively.

Sailing and fishing boats use pulleys and pulley systems to raise and lower sails and lift heavy nets and traps out of the water. Rock climbers use pulleys to lift heavy gear up steep cliffs. A bicycle's gears and chain are like a pulley system that helps a rider use less effort to move the bike, just as pulleys help lift heavy objects more easily.

The bike chain connects the front gear (attached to the pedals) and the back gear (attached to the wheel). When you pedal, the front gear turns the chain, which pulls the back gear and makes the wheel spin. This is how a pulley system uses a rope and wheel to move or lift a heavy object.

Would it be possible to build a skyscraper with no pulleys? In factories and on construction sites, pulleys are used to lift and move heavy objects. They are essential in cranes and other machinery used for heavy lifting. In all these examples, pulley systems distribute the weight of a load across multiple ropes, providing a mechanical advantage.

> **FULL STEAM**
>
> The Roman Colosseum had elevators for moving animals from the basement up to the arena floor.

Pulleys allow workers to safely and efficiently handle heavy loads with less physical exertion.

Pulleys are ingenious simple machines. By understanding the mechanical advantage and the relationship between force, distance, and work, we can see how pulleys make lifting heavy objects much easier. Whether in a fixed, moveable, or compound-pulley system, pulleys allow us to change the direction of force, reduce the required effort, and make work more efficient. Whether you're lifting a sail on a boat, using a crane on a construction site, or raising a curtain in a theater, pulleys are an essential part of our daily lives.

KEY QUESTIONS

- If pulleys had never been invented, do you think we'd have skyscrapers?
- Why does the wheel of the pulley need to have a lip on its edge?

VOCAB LAB

Write down what you think each word means. What root words can you find to help you? What does the context of the word tell you?

block and tackle, compound pulley, dumbwaiter, fixed pulley, isthmus, moveable pulley, and **segment**

Compare your definitions with those of your friends or classmates. Did you all come up with the same meanings? Turn to the text and glossary if you need help.

TEXT TO WORLD

Where do you encounter pulleys in your daily life? How do they make your life easier?

PULLEYS

Inquire & Investigate

LIFT A LOAD WITH A PULLEY

Pulleys are simple machines that make it easier to lift heavy objects. Fixed pulleys change the direction of a force, while moveable pulleys reduce the amount of force needed to lift an object. You can make both types of pulleys with a few household items!

- **Twist two pipe cleaners together to create one long pipe cleaner.** Slide the pipe cleaner through a spool. Secure the pipe cleaners to a closet rod or similar object so that the spool hangs below the rod. If you do not have a closet rod available, you can rest a broomstick horizontally across two chairs.

- **Fill a small bucket with marbles or other objects.** Lift the bucket with your hand. How heavy does it feel?

- **Attach one end of the string to the bucket's handle.** Run the string over the spool and let the other end of the string hang free. Pull down on the free end of the string to lift the bucket and its load. Was the pail easier or harder to lift than by hand?

- **What happens if you add a second pulley to your system?** This time, thread a pipe cleaner through a second spool and attach it to the bucket's handle. This forms a moveable pulley that moves with the load.

- **Attach one end of the string to the closet rod.** Loop the string under the moveable pulley and up and over the top of the fixed pulley.

- **Pull the free end of the string to raise the bucket.** Was the bucket easier or harder to lift with two pulleys?

Ideas for Supplies

- pipe cleaners
- several empty spools of thread or ribbon
- closet rod
- small bucket with a handle
- marbles, rocks, coins, or other objects to lift
- string, about 8 feet long

To investigate more, how can you make your pulley system lift more weight? Test a system with three or four pulleys. What happens?

56   ENGINEERING | CHAPTER THREE

DESIGN A BOOK LIFT

Inquire & Investigate

We use pulleys to lift heavy objects. In this activity, you'll put your engineering hat on to design and build a pulley system that can lift a paperback book 3 feet off the ground. You will use a variety of household materials to build your book lift.

Ideas for Supplies

- science notebook
- sample pulley materials
- paperback book
- spring weight (optional)

- **Gather materials to build a pulley system that can lift a paperback book three feet in the air.** For example, you might use spools, wooden dowels, pencils, paper towel tubes, pipe cleaners, string, rope, or metal wheels.

- **Sketch a design for a book lift in your science notebook.** How many pulleys will you use? How will you arrange them in the pulley system?

- **Build a prototype of the book lift and test how it works.** Did the lift successfully raise the book 3 feet? What improvements can you make to the design?

- **Compare your design to your classmates' designs.** Which design required the least effort to raise the book? Which design required the most effort? Why?

> To investigate more, adjust your design to add a counterweight to the pulley system. How does adding a counterweight affect the operation of the pulley?

PULLEYS 57

Chapter 4
Screws

What two simple machines make up a screw?

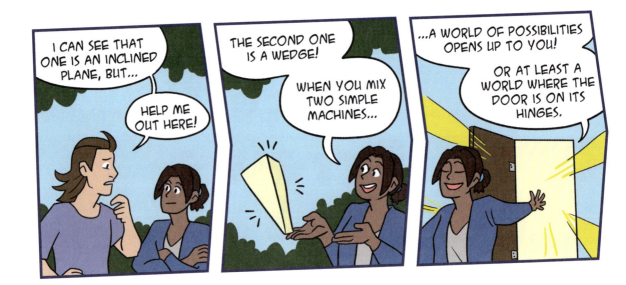

A screw is made of an inclined plane wrapped around a cylinder. The inclined plane is the thread that winds around in a spiral. On screws you find in a hardware store, the pointy tip is another simple machine—a wedge!

● ● ● ● ● ● ● ●

Have you ever built a piece of furniture? What tiny tools join the pieces to each other? Screws! A screw is a powerful, simple machine used to hold things together—they are some of the most widely used simple machines in the world. Screws hold together the parts of toys, furniture, computers, and much more. Screws even join large beams and other parts of buildings. This tiny tool twists and brings the world together like nothing else!

A screw is a twisted rod with a pointed end and a top called the head. Screw heads can be different shapes, such as round, stars, or even a plus sign. The screw's head is where you place a screwdriver to turn the screw.

The other end of the screw is sharp and pointed tip. As the screw turns, the point acts like a tiny knife to cut into the material such as wood or metal. The point is often tapered, making it easier for the screw to cut and penetrate a material.

60 ENGINEERING | CHAPTER FOUR

The screw's shaft extends from the screw's head to its point. A twisted ridge called a thread wraps around the shaft. You can think of a screw's thread as a spiral ramp that circles the shaft. The distance between threads is called the pitch. A screw's pitch is always the same on the same screw.

Screws come in all sizes and materials.

Each screw is designed for specific uses. For example, wood screws are designed to join wood pieces together. They usually have sharp points and threads to grip wood securely. Metal screws are used to join metal materials. Metal screws are usually harder and stronger than wood screws and may have finer threads that are better at gripping metal materials. There are some metal screws that are used with wood. Some kinds of screws aren't for building, but for moving large amounts of water or dirt. Those screws use the threads to shift material from one place to another.

HOW A SCREW WORKS

Screws can push or pull materials together. As with all simple machines, screws use mechanical advantage to make a task easier. What would happen if you tried to push a screw straight into a piece of wood? The screw probably would not penetrate the wood very deeply. What if you used a hammer to bang it in? That's not going to work, either! But what if you twist the screw into the wood? That's a much easier job! The more you twist, the deeper the screw moves into the material.

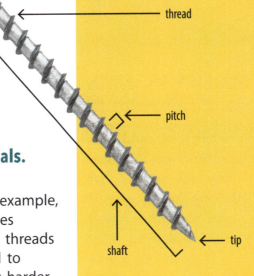

head
thread
pitch
tip
shaft

Most screws are used to fasten two materials together. Watch this video to better understand how they work. **What are the two parts of a screw?**

Next Gen Science screws

SCREWS 61

SCREWS VS. NUTS AND BOLTS

Like screws, nuts and bolts are fasteners that hold materials together, but they are not the same. A screw is a single fastener with threads along its entire length. Its sharp point twists into a material. In comparison, a nut and bolt are used together to fasten objects. The bolt has threads along part of its length but does not have a pointed end. Instead, the bolt fits through a drilled hole in a material. On the other side of the material, the nut fits over the end of the bolt and is screwed into place to tighten the bolt and secure an object in place.

● ● ● ● ● ● ● ● ● ●

If you look closely, the threads on a screw look a lot like another simple machine—the inclined plane.

Earlier, we explored how inclined planes make it easier to move a heavy object. If you try to lift a heavy box straight up, it can be very difficult. But if you push the box on a ramp, you can use less effort to move the box up to the target height. The ramp's inclined plane reduces your effort by spreading it over a longer distance.

A screw works similarly. When you turn a screw, you apply a force. The screw's threads are like a twisted inclined plane. They allow a smaller force to be applied over a longer distance. As you twist the screw, it turns a smaller rotational force into a much larger pushing or pulling force that drives the screw into a material. The more you twist the screw, the deeper it moves into the material. The screw's threads spread the applied force out over its threads, making it easier to drive the screw into the material.

FULL STEAM

Some screws are so tiny they can be used in watches, phones, and eyeglasses!

When you turn a screw, the twisting force you are using is torque. As you turn the screw, you apply torque to the head of the screw. This rotational force is transferred through the screw's threads to generate linear motion straight up and down along the screw's shaft. And the screw moves straight into the material.

Another kind of screw makes it easier to screw tops on bottles and lightbulbs into sockets. These screws aren't pushing aside material—instead, they're interacting with threads that are already there to keep the lid tight.

ENGINEERING | CHAPTER FOUR

MECHANICAL ADVANTAGE OF A SCREW

A screw provides a mechanical advantage because it changes the strength of the applied force, making it easier to perform a task. A screw converts rotational motion (turning the screw with a screwdriver) into linear motion (the screw moving into the material). When you turn a screw, you apply a smaller rotational force over a longer distance (the screw's threads) to get a greater force over a shorter distance (how far the screw pushes into the material). In this way, the screw reduces the effort needed to get the job done. Of course, we also have power tools that do a great job of screwing things in place. Mechanical advantage comes into play more when we're using our own two hands to do the work.

The mechanical advantage of a screw depends on the circumference of its head and its pitch. The head's circumference (C) is a measure of the distance around the screw in one full rotation. The screw's pitch (P) is a measure of how far the screw moves into the material with each rotation.

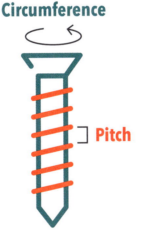

We can use this equation to calculate the mechanical advantage (MA) of a screw.

MA = Circumference / Pitch

JOHN LANDIS MASON

Have you ever stored food in a mason jar? If so, you can thank American inventor John Landis Mason (1832–1902)! In 1858, Mason invented the Mason jar, a glass jar that can be used to preserve food. The jar has a special screw-on lid with a rubber seal that keeps air out. This helps food last much longer. Before Mason's invention, it was hard to store food safely for a long time. With the Mason jar, people could safely store fruits, vegetables, and jams at home. The popular Mason jar is still used today! Does your family do any canning or other kinds of food preservation?

SCREWS

THE NUMBER PI

Pi (π) is a special number used in math, especially when working with circles. It shows the relationship between a circle's diameter, the distance across the middle of a circle, and its circumference, the distance around the circle's edge. When you divide the circle's circumference by its diameter, the answer is always the same: Pi (π) = 3.14. Pi is an irrational number. That means it goes on forever without repeating. Pi = 3.1415926535 . . . and it keeps going. But most of the time, we simply round it to 3.14. Do you celebrate Pi Day on March 14?

• • • • • • • • •

Let's calculate the mechanical advantage of a screw with a radius of 0.1 centimeter and 5 threads per centimeter.

We can use the radius of the screw head to calculate its circumference (C), or how far your hand travels to turn the screw one full rotation.

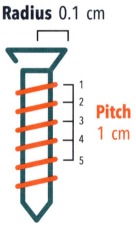

$$C = 2πr$$
$$C = 2π \times 0.1 \text{ cm}$$
$$C = 0.628$$

Next, calculate the pitch (P) of the screw. We know that the screw has five threads per centimeter.

$$P = 1 \text{ cm} / 5 \text{ threads}$$
$$P = 0.2 \text{ cm}$$

This is the linear distance the screw will travel into the material after one full rotation.

Finally, we can use the circumference (C) and pitch (P) to calculate the screw's mechanical advantage.

$$MA = C / P$$
$$MA = 0.628 / 0.2$$
$$MA = 3.14$$

This screw has a mechanical advantage of 3.14. It will produce an output force that is 3.14 times greater than the input force used to turn the screw.

How does mechanical advantage change if a screw's threads are closer together (a smaller pitch)?

Calculate the mechanical advantage of the screw if it has the same circumference but 10 threads per centimeter.

First, calculate the pitch.

P = 1 cm / 10 threads

P = 0.1 cm

Now, calculate the mechanical advantage.

MA = C / P

MA = 0.628 / 0.1

MA = 6.28

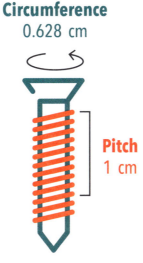

Circumference 0.628 cm

Pitch 1 cm

A screw with a smaller pitch has a greater mechanical advantage. The screw is easier to turn and takes less force to penetrate the material. The trade-off is that you'll have to turn it more times to finish the task because the input force must be applied over a greater distance.

FRICTION AND SCREWS

Have you ever tried to pry apart something held together with screws? It's nearly impossible. Why is a screw so good at holding things together? Screws are strong because of the way their threads work.

LIFTING OBJECTS

You can also use screws to lift a heavy load. A screw jack is a tool for lifting heavy objects such as cars. When you turn the jack's handle, it applies a rotational force to the screw. The screw turns the rotational motion into a linear motion that pushes a nut up and down the threaded screw. The nut lifts or lowers the car. The screw provides a mechanical advantage and allows a small input force to be multiplied into a greater output force that lifts the heavy car. The screw jack's threads create friction and prevent the nut from slipping on the screw.

● ● ● ● ● ● ● ●

SCREWS

The threads are like little hooks that grab onto the material—the wood, plastic, metal, or other material—they're being twisted into. When the screw goes into the material, the threads dig in and create a tight grip. This grip securely holds things together, much more strongly than other fasteners such as nails or glue.

> **FULL STEAM**
>
> A screwdriver is a tool designed to turn screws, making the job of using screws much easier. A screwdriver is also an example of another simple machine—a wheel and axle!

Screws are also strong because of friction. Friction is the force that resists motion when two objects rub against each other. As you turn and push a screw into a material, the screw creates friction. A screw usually generates more friction than a nail because its threads are in contact with a much greater surface area than a nail. The result is more friction. Greater friction helps a screw provide a stronger hold compared to a nail. The friction between the material and the screw's threads prevents the screw from becoming loose quickly. That is why screws are used to build many things, from toys to buildings.

SCREWS IN HISTORY

Take a look at this video to learn more about the history and importance of screws. **Why was it revolutionary to move skills from humans to machines?**

Machine Thinking where screws come from

The Ancient Greeks were some of the earliest users of the screw. They grew olives and grapes, which they crushed to make olive oil and wine. The Greeks used a machine called a press to crush these fruits. Wooden screws improved the design of these presses. Oil and winemakers placed the fruit between two pieces of wood or another material, connected by a screw. When they turned the screw, the wood pieces moved closer together, pressed the fruit, and allowed the juices to run out and be collected.

66 ENGINEERING | CHAPTER FOUR

Around 250 BCE, the Ancient Greek scientist and inventor Archimedes made a device based on a screw, now called the Archimedes's screw, to move water from a lower level to a higher level. This device is a spiral screw inside a cylinder. You place the lower end of the screw in the water source. As you turn a crank, the screw rotates. Water gets trapped in the threads and gradually moves to the top of the screw, where it is released at a higher level.

This screw-shaped machine was a simple but very effective tool for moving water upward. Today, the Archimedes's screw is still in use for irrigation, to lift water for rides in amusement parks, and to fill chocolate fountains.

During the 1400s, German inventor Johannes Gutenberg (c. 1393–1468) used screws to build a printing press, one of the world's most significant inventions. The press used screws to press paper against inked type with even pressure, which transferred the ink to the paper. The printing press meant printers could make multiple copies of books and documents quickly and efficiently.

This invention led to the mass production of books and the spread of knowledge worldwide.

LEADSCREWS

Leadscrews are a type of screw used in automated systems to move things in a straight line. A leadscrew looks like a long screw. When it turns, the leadscrew makes a nut or other part slide along the screw. The leadscrew turns its spinning motion into linear motion. The part moves in a straight line instead of spinning. The part can move in a straight line along one or more axes, such as left-right, up-down, or forward-backward. Leadscrews are used in machines such as 3D printers, robotics, and other manufacturing machines to move parts exactly where they need to go.

● ● ● ● ● ● ● ●

During the 1700s and 1800s, the Industrial Revolution swept across England, Europe, and the United States. Screws became essential for building and fastening machinery used in manufacturing, construction, transportation, and more.

For example, one notable machine, the steam engine, used screws throughout to fasten parts, pistons, and other components. The use of screws in machinery helped drive the Industrial Revolution, which paved the way for modern technologies in the 1900s and 2000s.

MAKING SCREWS

The earliest screws were made of wood and whittled by hand. Sometimes, craftspeople used manual lathes equipped with chisels or knives to make wooden screws. Later, craftspeople used files to make metal screws and shape the grooved threads. Making screws by hand was a time-consuming process, and the quality of the screw depended on the person making it. Each screw was different, and most were not interchangeable. What kinds of problems would this have created?

FULL STEAM

Screws were used in early firearms to hold the trigger mechanism, barrel, and stock together.

During the late 1700s, British toolmaker Henry Maudslay (1771–1831) built upon the earlier work of other toolmakers and developed an automated screw-cutting lathe. Maudslay's lathe created standardized screws and screw threads. As a result, it became possible for screws to be used interchangeably. During the next century, engineers invented machines to mass-produce standardized screws.

ENGINEERING | CHAPTER FOUR

The ability to mass-produce screws had a significant effect on manufacturing and engineering. With mass production, screws could be made faster and in greater quantities. Every screw was the exact same size and shape, making them interchangeable. A worn-out screw could be easily replaced with another one that was exactly the same. Machines became easier to build and repair as identical screws could be used in different machines and devices.

During the early 1900s, flathead screws were the most common type of screw. A flathead screw has a horizontal slot on its head. You place a screwdriver's flat end into this slot to turn the screw. People complained, however, that when twisting the screw, the screwdriver frequently slipped out of the slot. To solve this problem, a few innovators developed new screw head designs. Around 1908, Canadian P.L. Robertson (1879–1951) created a square-headed screw design that became popular in Canada. In that country, the Ford Model T car used more than 700 Robertson screws.

During the early 1930s, American businessman Henry Phillips (1889–1958) filed a patent for a screw design called the Phillips head screw. Phillips bought and improved an early version of the design from a laborer named John Thompson. At the time, car manufacturers such as Ford and General Motors needed screws that could withstand greater torque and provide more secure fastenings. The new Phillips head screw was the perfect solution. Phillips invited General Motors to test his new screw design in the 1936 Cadillac. All U.S. automakers eventually used the Phillips head screw on their assembly lines.

While we now have different types of screwheads, you'll still see many flathead screws in the world!

PROPELLERS

The propeller on an airplane or ship is a type of screw. The curved blades of the propeller are like the threads of a screw. The propeller rotates and converts its rotational motion into linear movement. An airplane's propeller moves the air and pulls the plane forward. A ship's propeller moves water and pushes the ship forward. The first large steamship powered by a screw propeller was built in 1838 and named the *SS Archimedes*. In the air, Orville Wright (1871–1948) and Wilbur Wright (1867–1912) completed the first propeller-powered flight in 1903. Today, propellers help move ships and airplanes every day.

SCREWS

This kind of screw moves a lot of dirt!

SCREWS TODAY

Today, screws are used throughout everyday life, in everything from construction to medicine. Modern screws come in different types, sizes, and materials for use in specific tasks. In construction, screws fasten wood, metal, and drywall, providing a strong and reliable hold for homes, schools, offices, and other structures. In the automotive and aerospace industries, screws hold together complex machinery and components. These screws are typically made of high-strength materials such as stainless steel or titanium to withstand extreme conditions.

FULL STEAM

The development of power tools has made driving screws into materials faster and more efficient.

ENGINEERING | CHAPTER FOUR

Electronics also rely heavily on screws for assembling devices such as computers, smartphones, and televisions. Tiny screws secure circuit boards, screens, batteries, and other internal components.

Screws are also common in furniture assembly, where they make it easy to build and take apart everything from a table to a bookcase.

Not all screws are used to fasten material to other material. Have you ever seen a dig site where workers are drilling into the earth? This kind of work is done with an auger. An auger is a kind of screw that moves dirt from one end to the other, similar to how water moves in an Archimedes's screw.

Augers can be small enough to be operated by hand or enormous enough to dig through many feet of dirt.

Screws are fascinating simple machines that help us do all types of essential work. They're used in almost everything we use daily, from toys and furniture to machines and electronics. By turning a screw, we can move things, hold things together, and make sure things stay in place. We wouldn't be able to build many of the items we rely on every day without the screw.

VOCAB LAB

Write down what you think each word means. What root words can you find to help you? What does the context of the word tell you?

Archimedes's screw, circumference, cylinder, interchangeable, lathe, linear motion, mass production, piston, pitch, radius, rotational motion, and **whittle**

Compare your definitions with those of your friends or classmates. Did you all come up with the same meanings? Turn to the text and glossary if you need help.

TEXT TO WORLD

What are some things in your home or classroom that are held together by screws?

KEY QUESTIONS

- Why is a circular staircase considered a type of screw?

- Why does a screw hold a wooden structure together more securely than a nail?

SCREWS 71

Inquire & Investigate

Ideas for Supplies

- PVC pipe, at least 1-inch diameter
- clear vinyl tubing, at least ¼-inch diameter
- duct tape
- scissors
- 2 bowls
- water
- blocks or other items to elevate one bowl

> To investigate more, adjust the design of the Archimedes's screw. What happens if you change the spiral spacing on the PVC pipe? How does that affect the function of the screw? What if you change the diameter of the PVC pipe or vinyl tubing? Does that affect how the screw works?

LIFT WATER WITH AN ARCHIMEDES'S SCREW

During the third century BCE, inventor and scientist Archimedes designed a massive ship at the request of the Greek king. However, the ship had a problem. It leaked water. Archimedes set out to find a way to remove that water. He invented a tool called the Archimedes's screw to remove the water from the ship. As we learned earlier in this chapter, the Archimedes's screw was a type of pump that could transport water from a lower place to a higher place. The Archimedes's screw was also easy for one person to operate. In this activity, you'll build a model of the Archimedes's screw and test how it works.

- **Tape one end of the vinyl tubing to one end of the PVC pipe.**

- **Tightly wrap the tubing in a spiral up the PVC pipe.** Use duct tape to attach the tubing to the other end of the PVC pipe. Cut off any excess tubing with scissors. Use a few pieces of tape to secure the spiraled tubing to the body of the PVC pipe if needed.

- **Fill one bowl with water.** Place it on a tabletop or flat surface. Water might spill during this activity, so choose a location that is easy to clean up.

- **Place the second, empty bowl on the tabletop.** Place a book or block under it so the second bowl is higher than the first bowl.

- **Place one end of the Archimedes's screw in the bowl with water.** Make sure the other end of the screw is over the higher bowl.

72   ENGINEERING | CHAPTER FOUR

Inquire & Investigate

- **Rotate the screw so the vinyl tubing scoops water from the bowl with each rotation.** The tubing's end should move under the water's surface and then rise above the surface with each rotation. If your screw does not appear to be picking up water, check to make sure you are rotating it in the proper direction.

- **Continue to rotate the screw.** Watch the water move up the tubing and flow into the higher bowl.

- **Raise the height of the second bowl so the screw tilts at a steeper angle.** How does the screw work when you are moving water even higher? Is there a point where the water no longer moves upward? Explain your findings.

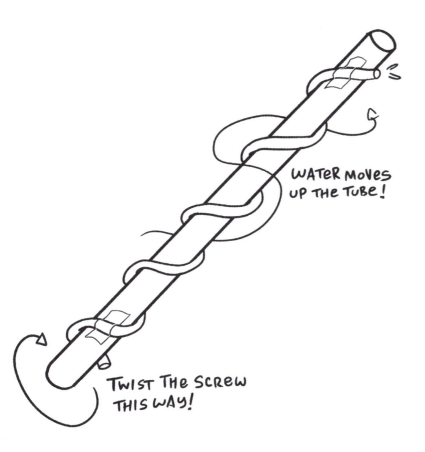

WATER MOVES UP THE TUBE!

TWIST THE SCREW THIS WAY!

RESEARCH!

How are screws used in the construction industry? On airplanes? In drilling for oil and natural gases? Do some research and create a presentation about the different ways screws are used in various types of industries.

• • • • • • • • •

SCREWS 73

Inquire & Investigate

Ideas for Supplies

- construction paper
- pencil
- ruler
- colored marker
- scissors
- tape

To investigate more, cut two new paper triangles—each with a different slope. Wrap each triangle around a same-sized pencil. How many lines (threads) are around each pencil? Which one will provide a greater mechanical advantage? Explain.

A SCREW'S INCLINED PLANE

A screw uses an inclined plane wrapped around a central rod to make work easier. In this activity, we'll make a paper screw to illustrate how this works.

- **Measure and mark 5 inches along the short side of the construction paper.** Measure and mark 9 inches along the long side of the paper. Use a ruler and draw a line connecting the two marks to form a right triangle.

- **Use a colored marker and ruler to draw a thick line along the triangle's longest edge.** Cut the triangle from the paper along the line. The triangle should look like a ramp or inclined plane.

- **Cut a second identical triangle from another piece of construction paper.** Make sure to use the colored marker to mark the triangle's longest edge.

- **Hold the short, vertical side of the triangle alongside a pencil.** Tape it in place.

- **Carefully wrap the triangle around the pencil.** The colored edge of the triangle should wind around the pencil like the threads of a screw. Tape the point down.

- **Wrap the second triangle around the thick marker.**

  - How many lines (threads) are around your pencil?
  - How many are around the thicker marker?
  - How does the number of lines affect how each paper screw works?
  - Which one will provide a greater mechanical advantage? Explain.

74 | ENGINEERING | CHAPTER FOUR

Chapter 5
Wedges

How does a wedge act to both break things apart and hold things together?

The shape of a wedge works to split material. You can also use a wedge to keep something, such as a door, from moving.

● ● ● ● ● ● ● ●

The wedge is one of the oldest simple machines. Have you cut an apple with a knife? Have you used a doorstop to hold a door open? Have you pushed a nail into a block of wood? If you answered yes to any of these questions, then you've used a wedge!

A wedge is a triangular-shaped object with two slanted sides that meet to form a sharp edge. A wedge can also be a cylinder that comes to a point. When you apply force to the wide, flat part of the wedge, the wedge's sharp edge cuts into or splits things. A wedge is a tool that multiplies force and changes its direction, making it easier to do specific jobs such as cutting, splitting, or separating objects.

Let's look at what a wedge is and how it helps to make tasks easier.

THE WEDGE AS A SIMPLE MACHINE

An axe is an example of how a wedge can make work easier. Imagine you need to split a log into several pieces that will fit better in the fireplace. Can you split the wood with your hands? That's probably impossible. What if you tried banging on the log with a hammer? Again, it will still be challenging to split the log.

Now, what happens if you use an axe to split the log? The axe's head has two slanted sides that form a sharp edge. When you swing an axe, it comes down on the wood log with force. The force you apply to the axe's wide, flat side is transferred to the axe's sharp edge. The axe's sharp edge pushes into the log and forces it to split apart.

HOW DOES IT WORK?

When you push or hit a wedge, you apply an input force. You might hit a chisel with a hammer, swing an axe, or push a knife into an ice cream cake. The wedge multiplies your input force into a larger output force. When you apply force to the wide, flat part of the wedge, it is directed down its sloped sides to the sharp edge. The wedge's sharp edge is smaller than its broad, flat side so the wedge concentrates the applied force to the smaller area. The sharper the wedge's edge, the smaller the area where the force concentrates.

The wedge also converts the concentrated force into two components, or directions. One component pushes the wedge's sharp edge deeper into the material. The other component pushes the material apart. The two components of the output force are strong enough to split the material.

THE PLOW AS A WEDGE

A plow is a farming tool based on a wedge. Its pointed, triangular blade is designed to cut through soil. When a plow moves forward, the sharp edge of the blade (wedge) splits and lifts the soil, making it easier to turn over. The narrow tip of the wedge concentrates force into a smaller area, allowing the plow to break apart the soil with less effort. This wedge shape is essential for the plow to work efficiently. It allows farmers to prepare soil for planting efficiently and effectively.

WEDGES

Watch this video from *The Highland Woodworker* to learn why the wedge is an important tool in the woodworking studio. **How does the wedge help hold materials together in woodworking?**

Rogowski Wedge

Have you ever seen a chisel? A chisel is a tool used to carve or cut materials such as wood or stone. When you hit the top of a chisel with a hammer, the applied force is distributed across the broad, flat top of the chisel. This force is transferred down the chisel's sloped sides to its smaller sharp edge. The force concentrates on the smaller area, exerting a greater force on the material being cut (wood or stone). It drives the chisel's sharp edge into the material. It also creates a sideways force that pushes the material apart.

What about a doorstop? Wedges are excellent at holding doors open or closed! The top side of the wedge can be jammed under the door, while the other side is held against the floor with friction. As the door applies pressure on the top side, that increases the amount of force going toward the floor.

FULL STEAM

Your front teeth are wedges! Every time you take a bite of an apple, your teeth split it into smaller pieces.

A WEDGE AND MECHANICAL ADVANTAGE

Splitting wood or other materials is often difficult—a wedge can make it much more manageable.

A wedge provides a mechanical advantage to make work easier. The wedge strengthens the input force and changes its direction, making splitting or cutting material easier. A wedge enables you to use less force to split something.

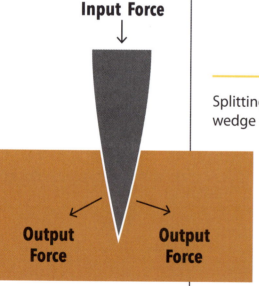

78   ENGINEERING | CHAPTER FIVE

A wedge's mechanical advantage depends on two factors:

- the length of the wedge's sloped sides (L)
- the width of the wedge (w)

We can calculate a wedge's mechanical advantage (MA) using this equation.

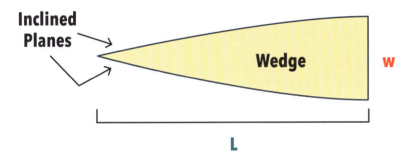

MA = length of wedge / width of wedge

This equation shows that a wedge with a longer (greater) length and sharper (smaller) width will have a greater mechanical advantage. Less force is needed to cut the material, making the task easier.

Knowing this relationship, engineers can design a wedge to produce the desired mechanical advantage by changing its length and width.

$$MA = L / w$$
$$MA = 9 / 3$$
$$MA = 3$$

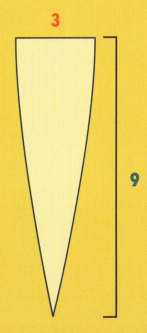

WEDGES 79

A SAFER WAY TO CHOP

Ayla Hutchinson from New Zealand was just 13 years old when her mother hurt her fingers using an axe. Hutchinson wanted to find a safer way to split firewood. She designed a tool that flips the axe and its wedge-shaped blade upside down. Her invention, the Kindling Cracker, made it safer and easier to chop firewood. It quickly became a worldwide success. In 2018, New Zealand honored Hutchinson and her invention with a commemorative postage stamp.

● ● ● ● ● ● ● ●

WEDGES IN HISTORY

People have been using wedges for thousands of years. Early humans used wedges to chop, cut, and shape wood, bone, and stone. Flint tools were sharp-edged, wedge-shaped stones that cut meat, carved wood, or split materials.

Early humans created wedges by chipping stones to sharpen the stones' edges.

One of history's most famous uses of a wedge is the axe, a tool used to chop wood for thousands of years—and still used today. In ancient civilizations, axes were made from stone or bronze. Later, they were made with iron and steel. Axes were used to clear forests for agriculture, build shelters, and cut firewood. Chisels were used to hollow out boats from logs.

Wedges have been used for thousands of years in construction projects. Archaeologists believe that workers in ancient civilizations in Egypt, Greece, and Rome used wedges to build massive temples, pyramids, and monuments. In Ancient Egypt, workers used wooden wedges to split massive limestone blocks. They inserted wooden wedges into cracks in the stone and poured water over the wedges. The soaked wood expanded and forced the limestone to split.

In Ancient China and India, wedges were commonly used to split large stones and logs. Workers hammered metal or wooden wedges into cracks in the stone. The large slabs of stone would gradually split into smaller blocks that could be used to build temples, palaces, and monuments.

ENGINEERING | CHAPTER FIVE

Wedges were also used in plows and other farming tools. Iron wedge-shaped blades broke up hard soil so farmers could prepare their fields for planting.

Wedges have also been used on the battlefield. Many ancient cultures, from the Egyptians to the Romans, used weapons with wedge-shaped blades, such as swords and knives, in battle. The wedge shape of these weapons made them efficient at cutting the enemy's armor—and flesh. Spears with wedge-shaped tips could also do a lot of damage.

Artists throughout history have used wedges as chisels to create intricate carvings and detailed sculptures. The Ancient Egyptians used chisels to carve symbols called hieroglyphics into stone. Artists also used chisels to cut intricate stone carvings on Gothic cathedrals. Italian artist Michelangelo (1475–1564) used chisels to carve his famous *David* sculpture from a single block of white marble. Modern artists use chisels to create various works, from jewelry to large statues.

> ## FULL STEAM
>
> Some golf clubs are called wedges because of their wedge-like shape.

During the 1700s and 1800s, pioneers in North America used wedge-shaped axes and tools to split logs to build log cabin homes and split-rail fences that enclosed fields and kept livestock secure. These early structures were a critical part of the establishment of the United States as a country.

WOW, WEDGES!

You can also use a wedge to lift an object or hold it in place. A doorstop is an example of a wedge that holds a door in place. Wedges can also fasten and secure materials together. How does that work? When a wedge is driven between two materials, it pushes them apart. Think about how this can work with a wedge-shaped doorstop. The doorstop creates pressure between the door's bottom and the floor, which holds the door in place. Builders also use wedges to secure stone or wood. They push a wedge into a crack or gap in the stone or wood. The wedge creates pressure that holds the materials and prevents them from moving.

Watch this video from the National Air and Space Museum to see how wedges are used in flight. **What is an airfoil and how does it help an aircraft fly?**

Smithsonian Air and Space wedges

During the 1900s, wedges continued to be important tools in many industries. Wedge-shaped parts helped secure machine components in factories. In hospitals, wedge-shaped tools helped doctors cut and separate tissue and adjust bones.

In transportation, engineers used wedges in engines and brake systems to apply pressure or hold parts in place.

WEDGES AT WORK

Today, wedges still make challenging tasks such as cutting wood or opening something much more manageable. Without wedges, we would need much more effort to split things apart. Wedges are used in many tools and machines to help with many tasks, from cutting food to building houses. Look around your house. How many wedges can you find?

One of the most common uses of a wedge is to cut or split materials.

The sharp edge of a wedge enables it to exert a force to separate materials along lines of weakness. For example, a knife is a small, handheld wedge used to cut food or other materials. The knife's sharp edge separates the material quickly. When you press the sharp edge of a knife into an apple, the force you apply to the handle is concentrated in the sharp edge and enables it to push through the fruit quickly.

Large industrial wedges separate and split large rocks or stone slabs in construction and mining.

FULL STEAM

The bow, or front, of a ship is a wedge. It splits and pushes water out of the way as the ship moves forward.

ENGINEERING | CHAPTER FIVE

A wedge is inserted into cracks or natural fractures in the rock and driven in, which splits the rock or stone into smaller pieces.

Wedges are also used to drive objects into materials. For example, a nail is an example of a wedge. The nail's broad, flat head tapers into a sharp point. When you hit the nail head with a hammer, the force travels down the nail and concentrates at its sharp point, allowing it to penetrate and split the material. Even though the nail is pushing material away from its tip, it's a tool used to hold things together. When you fasten a sign to a post with a nail, you are using friction to keep those elements pressed against each other.

Wedges also hold things together. A tent stake is a type of wedge that drives into the ground and holds tent ropes tight. A staple is a wedge that pushes through paper and holds several sheets together. A keystone is a wedge-shaped stone that holds an arch together. The keystone applies pressure to the stones on either side of it, causing them to press tightly against each other. The pressure locks the stones into place, preventing them from moving.

A wedge is a simple machine that helps you cut, split, or separate things by using a sharp point to focus the force you apply. A wedge also exerts pressure that can be used to hold materials together. It's a tool that makes challenging tasks easier by changing the direction and strength of the force you apply. Using a wedge will make the job easier!

KEY QUESTIONS

- **What would eating be like without wedge-shaped teeth?**
- **How are simple machines important in art as well as in engineering?**

VOCAB LAB

Write down what you think each word means. What root words can you find to help you? What does the context of the word tell you?

bow, concentrate, durable, flint, fracture, hieroglyphics, limestone, and **pioneer**

Compare your definitions with those of your friends or classmates. Did you all come up with the same meanings? Turn to the text and glossary if you need help.

TEXT TO WORLD

What other simple machines act to both bring material together and split it apart?

WEDGES

Inquire & Investigate

WEDGES AT WORK

The bow of a boat is usually wedge-shaped to make it easier for the boat to move through the water. In this activity, you'll test this concept.

- **Place the bin on a flat surface.** Fill it with rice or sand.
- **Attach a pushpin to each block.**
- **Place the rectangular block in the bin at one end.** Make sure it is surrounded by the rice and not just sitting on top of it.
- **Attach the spring scale to the block and pull it through the rice.** Note the force measurement on the spring scale and record it in your science notebook.
- **Re-spread the rice in the bin and pull the wedge-shaped block through the rice.** Record the force measurement.
- **Which block needed more force to move through the rice?** Why?

Ideas for Supplies

- a large rectangular bin or baking pan filled with dry rice or sand
- a rectangular or square block
- a wedge-shaped block
- pushpins
- spring scale
- science notebook

To investigate more, repeat the experiment with different-shaped blocks. Record your results. How does the object's shape affect the force required to pull it through the rice?

ENGINEERING | CHAPTER FIVE

THE SHAPE OF A WEDGE

Inquire & Investigate

A wedge makes work easier by strengthening and changing the direction of an input force. The wedge is a two-sided version of an inclined plane that splits material apart. The sharper the edge of the wedge, the less force is needed to split the material. In this activity, you'll see how the shape of a wedge affects how it works.

- **Use a protractor and ruler to draw three double wedges on a piece of heavy cardboard.** A double wedge looks like two inclined planes placed back-to-back. Wedge #1 should have an angle of 20 degrees, Wedge #2 an angle of 40 degrees, and Wedge #3 an angle of 60 degrees.

- **Cut each wedge from the cardboard.** Attach a paper clip to the tip of each wedge.

- **Place two large books side by side on a flat surface.** The books should be touching.

- **Use a spring scale to pull Wedge #1 between the two books.** What force is needed to separate the books? Repeat this twice with Wedge #1. Record your data and observations in your science notebook.

- **Repeat three times each with Wedge #2 and Wedge #3.** Record your data and observations.

- **Create a table with your data.** What is the average force needed for each wedge? Which wedge required the least amount of force to move the books? Which required the most force? Why?

Ideas for Supplies

- heavy cardboard
- protractor
- ruler
- pencil
- scissors
- paper clips
- spring scale
- two large books
- science notebook

To investigate more, consider how the thickness of the wedge affects your results. Repeat this activity and measure how far apart each wedge moved the books. Which wedge moved the books the farthest apart? Explain. How is this knowledge useful for engineers?

WEDGES | 85

Inquire & Investigate

WHICH WEDGE WORKS BEST?

Wedges come in different sizes and angles and can be made from different materials. Engineers use their knowledge of how wedges work to design the right wedge for the job. In this activity, you'll test different wedges and materials. You'll gather information to help with wedge design and material selection.

Ideas for Supplies

- several wedges of different sizes and materials
- science notebook
- bar of soap
- block of clay
- Styrofoam block
- foam block (such as that found in flower arrangements)

- **Gather several wedges of different sizes and materials.** For example, you might choose a hardwood wedge, a balsa wood wedge, a plastic knife, or similar items.

- **Create a data table for the experiment in your science notebook.**

- **Test how Wedge #1 works to separate each of the target materials.** Write your observations in the data table. Think about the following questions.

  - Does the wedge separate the target material well? Are the edges rough or smooth?
  - Does the wedge break when you try to use it?
  - If the wedge cannot separate the material, can it dent it?

- **Repeat the tests on the target materials using the other wedges.**

- **What type of wedge worked the best on each target material?** Which wedge was the least successful on each target material? Which wedge was most durable? Which was the least durable?

- **How could you use this information to design a wedge for an engineering project?**

To investigate more, try separating your target materials with natural wedges—a stone, stick, or something else you find outside. What's different?

ENGINEERING | CHAPTER FIVE

Chapter 6
Wheels and Axles

What would life be like without the wheel and axle?

Without the wheel and axle, it would be a lot harder to travel farther than your neighborhood! Cars, bikes, and wagons all operate on wheels.

● ● ● ● ● ● ● ●

The wheel and axle work together as a simple machine that makes things turn. Wheels and axles are in action whenever you ride a bike or skate on rollerblades. You wouldn't get very far in a car or bus without wheels and axles. Imagine shopping at the grocery store without a wheeled cart—carrying all your snacks would be much more work!

The wheel and axle make up a simple but incredibly powerful simple machine that has transformed our daily lives. The invention of the wheel and axle thousands of years ago allowed humans to develop all sorts of things, from transportation to machines. Today, we use the wheel and axle in countless ways to make life easier.

The wheel is a circular object that rotates around a central point. Wheels come in all sizes, from the tiny wheels on toy cars to the massive wheels on monster trucks to Ferris wheels. Wheels can be made of different materials, such as rubber, metal, or wood.

ENGINEERING | CHAPTER SIX

Wheels are all around us. Steering wheels, doorknobs, drills, car tires, and electric fans are all examples of wheels.

A wheel works with an axle, which is a rod that runs through the wheel's center. The wheel rotates around the axle. Most of the time, the wheel and axle are attached and turn in the same direction. Together, the wheel and axle can lift heavy objects or move materials and people.

Do you use a pizza cutter on pizza nights? That's another use for a wheel! A spinning wheel is an important textile tool and no baker would be without a rolling pin—both wheels. Wheels and axles can also be parts of larger machines such as steam rollers, wind turbines, and tunnel-boring machines, which cut huge holes through deep rock using a rotating cutter wheel.

PENNY-FARTHING BICYCLES

A bigger wheel produces a greater mechanical advantage. During the late 1800s, the penny-farthing bicycle attempted to create an even greater mechanical advantage than other bicycles of the time by using a very large front wheel. The bike's front wheel was about 5 feet in diameter, while its back wheel was much smaller. A pair of pedals were attached to the large front wheel where the rider sat. With each rotation of the pedals, the large wheel made a full rotation and covered a large distance. The penny-farthing bike was popular because it was faster than bicycles with smaller wheels. But it was difficult to balance on and could be dangerous if you fell from the high seat. Eventually, safer bicycles with equal-sized wheels replaced the penny-farthing bicycle.

● ● ● ● ● ● ● ●

WHEELS AND AXLES

HOW THEY WORK

Just as with all simple machines, force is an important part of how a wheel and axle work. The wheel and axle turn together in the same direction when a force is applied to either part. They rotate around a central point called a fulcrum at the same rate and complete one full rotation at the same time. However, the wheel and axle are different sizes. That means the distance each one travels in one rotation is different.

A larger wheel travels a greater distance than the smaller axle.

Sometimes, as in cars or bicycles, a force is applied to the axle. The rotation of the axle is transferred to the wheel. Because the wheel is larger than the axle, the wheel moves a greater distance with each rotation. This efficiently moves the car or bicycle wheels along the road until the driver applies the brakes and friction brings the vehicle to a stop.

Let's look more closely at the wheels on a car. The car's engine generates a force that turns the axles. The axles rotate the car's wheels. Because the wheels are larger than the axles, they move farther than the axle in one complete rotation. This creates movement to propel the car forward.

In other examples, a small force is applied to the wheel. The input force is multiplied into a greater force that turns the axle. The axle moves a shorter distance but turns with greater force. The wheel and axle work together to multiply force. Just as a lever multiplies a linear force, the wheel and axle multiply a rotational force.

Watch this video from Next Generation Science and see some examples of wheels and axles in daily life. Which everyday wheel and axle have you used?

Next Gen wheel axle

FULL STEAM

Roads in Ancient Rome were typically 13.8 feet wide, providing just enough space for two carts or chariots with wheels to pass each other.

---

90 | ENGINEERING | CHAPTER SIX

You can see this in action with a car's steering wheel. The force applied to turn the steering wheel is multiplied by the car's wheel-and-axle system, allowing you to steer the car with a relatively small input force.

A doorknob is another example of a wheel and axle mechanism. The rounded knob acts as a wheel, while the shaft that extends into the door is the axle. When you turn the knob, it rotates the shaft to open the latch on the door.

You can use less force to work the knob because the wheel and axle multiplies this force to turn the shaft.

Have you ever seen a wind turbine? The input force from the wind pushes the turbine's blades, which act as a wheel. The blades rotate around a central shaft, or axle. The wheel is much larger than the axle, so the wheel travels a much greater distance with each rotation than the axles. The axle rotates a smaller distance but with greater force.

WHEELS AND FRICTION

As we learned earlier, when two surfaces rub together, the result is friction. Friction opposes motion and acts in the opposite direction. When you slide a heavy box on the ground, you encounter a lot of friction between the box and the ground. The friction pushes against your motion, making it much harder to slide the box. But what happens if you put the box on wheels?

When you roll the box, only a tiny part of the wheels' surface touches the ground at any point. A much smaller surface area rubs against the ground. Less friction! And less work for you.

SPINNING WHEELS

The spinning wheel revolutionized how textiles were produced. Some of the first spinning wheels appeared in India around 500 to 1000 CE. Early spinning wheels also appeared in Asia, the Middle East, and Europe. The spinning wheel made it much easier and faster to spin fibers such as cotton, wool, or flax into thread or yarn that could be used to weave cloth. To use a spinning machine, a person turned a larger wheel called a drive wheel either by hand or with pedals. The drive band connected the wheel to a flyer, which twisted the fibers to form thread. The finished thread wound onto a bobbin.

WHEELS AND AXLES

GEARING UP

Many machines use gears to transfer movement and force between different parts of the machine. A gear is like a wheel with teeth around its edge. The gear's teeth, which are levers, are made to fit with the teeth of another gear. The gear is typically mounted on an axle, which allows it to rotate. When one gear rotates, its teeth push against the teeth of the second gear, which causes the second gear to rotate in the opposite direction. Many gears can be connected, all different shapes and sizes. The size of the gear affects how it works. A smaller gear rotates faster but with less force. A larger gear rotates more slowly but with more force. Gears use their teeth to transfer the turning motion (from the wheel and axle) from one part to another, changing speed and force to make machines work efficiently.

Plus, rolling friction is less forceful than sliding friction. Wheels convert sliding friction into rolling friction, making it easier to move objects. When less friction pushes against your box, you need less effort to move it.

The material used to make a wheel also plays a role in reducing friction. Modern car tires are made with special rubber compounds that reduce rolling friction. Less rolling friction means the wheel takes less energy to roll over a surface. For a car, that means it needs less fuel to travel a certain distance. But tires need to have some friction, or grip, with the road to prevent the car from sliding too much, especially in wet or icy conditions. Engineers design tire tread patterns to grip the road better in rain or snow, while other treads are smoother for dry roads.

Wheel technology can also reduce friction with the road. For example, alloy wheels are made from a mixture of aluminum and other metals. They are lighter than steel wheels, which lowers the overall car weight. A lighter car experiences less friction with the road, making it easier to move and stop. Engineers are always exploring new ways to improve wheel technology and make vehicles safer and more efficient.

CALCULATING MECHANICAL ADVANTAGE

The wheel and axle make work easier by providing mechanical advantage in three primary ways: covering a greater distance using less force, multiplying rotational force, and reducing friction during movement.

ENGINEERING | CHAPTER SIX

As a result of this mechanical advantage, the wheel and axle make it easier to move heavy objects or travel across distances. The mechanical advantage (MA) of a wheel and axle can be calculated by comparing the wheel's radius to the axle's radius. We can use the following formula.

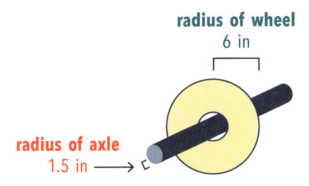

MA = radius of wheel / radius of axle

For example, a wheel and axle work to lift a bucket of water from a deep well. The wheel has a radius of 6 inches, and the axle has a radius of 1.5 inches. We can calculate the mechanical advantage of this simple machine.

MA = radius of wheel / radius of axle

MA = 6 inches / 1.5 inches

MA = 4

In this scenario, when you use 1 newton of force to turn the wheel, the wheel and axle provide 4 newtons of force to lift the bucket of water.

Watch this video from PBS to learn how gears work on a bicycle. **How can changing a bike's gear help you pedal up a steep hill?**

PBS Design Squad bicycle gears

WHEELS AND AXLES 93

What if you used a bigger wheel with a 12-inch radius? How does that affect mechanical advantage?

MA = radius of wheel / radius of axle

MA = 12 inches / 1.5 inches

MA = 8

Increasing the size of the wheel increases the mechanical advantage. The larger the wheel, the easier it is to lift or move heavy objects.

WHEELS IN HISTORY

People have been using wheels and axles for thousands of years. Archaeologists believe that humans began using wheels and axles independently in several ancient civilizations. Some of the earliest archaeological records of wheels come from Mesopotamia—the area known as modern-day Iraq—around 3500 BCE. These early wheels were not used for transportation. They were potter's wheels, which craftspeople used to create and shape different types of vessels made of clay.

Around 3000 BCE, some of the first wheeled carts appeared. The wheels were solid wooden disks attached to their axles. These wheeled carts made it much easier to move people and goods over long distances. So much better than walking or carrying goods by hand!

Ancient potter's wheels were moved by sticks or feet. Now, most potter's wheels are electric.

ENGINEERING | CHAPTER SIX

As more people used wheels, they improved the design. A solid wooden wheel was heavy and slow. So people designed a wheel with wooden spokes radiating from a central hub. The spoked wheel was lighter and faster than solid wooden wheels.

In Ancient Egypt, farmers used wheeled vehicles for agriculture, and the military built wheeled chariots to carry soldiers and supplies in battle.

Wheeled carts and other vehicles transported the materials to build Egypt's pyramids and other structures. The Ancient Greeks and Romans also refined the wheel. The Romans built a network of roads on which wheeled vehicles could travel.

FULL STEAM

Wheelwrights were highly skilled craftspeople who designed and built wheels.

The first wheelbarrows appeared in China around 100 CE, during the Han Dynasty. Many early Chinese wheelbarrows had a single wheel directly under the load. This design helped people balance and transport heavy loads. Farmers used wheelbarrows to carry crops, tools, and supplies across their fields. Builders used wheelbarrows to move heavy building materials. Soldiers also used wheelbarrows to move supplies, weapons, and injured soldiers during battles.

During the Middle Ages, the use of the wheel continued to expand. People built waterwheels to capture the force of flowing water to make it easier to grind grain into flour. Windmills and clocks operated with wheel-and-axle systems.

The Industrial Revolution of the 1700s and 1800s brought a massive leap in how wheels were designed and used.

ANCIENT WHEEL

The Ljubljana Marshes Wheel is the oldest wooden wheel discovered to date. It is about 5,000 years old and was discovered by archaeologists in 2002 in the Ljubljana Marshes in Slovenia. The wheel was made from ash wood, and its axle was made from oak. It was likely part of a simple, two-wheeled cart used by people who lived in the region around 3000 BCE.

WHEELS AND AXLES 95

During the Industrial Revolution, innovations such as the steam engine, railroads, and automobiles all relied heavily on the wheel and axle. Wheels and axles became essential parts of factory machinery, locomotives, steam engines, and automobiles.

By the late 1800s and early 1900s, wheel design changed to make cars and other vehicles safer, stronger, and easier to operate.

An Islamic water wheel that once raised water to the caliph's palace

Most vehicles used wooden or spoke wheels with rubber tires. The invention of air-filled tires in 1888 made rides smoother.

During the 1920s, steel wheels became popular because they were stronger. The alloy wheels of the 1980s and 1990s were lighter, which made vehicles more fuel efficient and easier to control.

THE WHEEL TODAY

Today, the wheel and axle are a crucial part of daily life. The wheel and axle are used in many vehicles, from cars and trucks to trains and buses. Airplanes use wheels and axles in their landing gear, enabling them to make smooth takeoffs and landings.

96 ENGINEERING | CHAPTER SIX

Wheels have even been used in space, with vehicles such as the Lunar Roving Vehicle traveling on the moon's surface on wheels. Even farther away, Mars rovers use wheels to travel the surface of another planet!

Wheels are essential in factories that manufacture everything from toys to appliances. They are part of gears, conveyor belts, machines, pulleys, and more. These technologies rely on wheel-and-axle systems to efficiently move materials and operate machinery.

The wheel and axle continue to drive innovation and have been used in cutting-edge technologies for robotics, renewable energy systems, and more.

Wheels are all around us. They have an enormous role in our daily lives. Wheels help us in transportation, machinery, tools, sports, and entertainment.

Can you imagine watching the Indy 500 if there were no wheels? In airports, even luggage has wheels!

The wheel is one of the most important inventions in human history. It makes work easier, transportation faster, and daily life more convenient. By understanding how a wheel and axle work, we can appreciate the simple but powerful physics principles behind this simple machine.

Whether you use wheels to ride a bike, drive a car, or move heavy objects, the wheels make a huge difference. And wheels will be a key part of technology in the future!

SHAPE-CHANGING WHEELS

Scientists and engineers are working to develop shape-changing wheels, also called morphing wheels. These advanced wheels can change their shape to adapt to different surfaces or driving conditions. For example, engineers are working on a morphing wheel that can adjust its stiffness to allow it to easily roll over obstacles. For people in wheelchairs, this type of wheel could make it easier to move over all types of terrain. Scientists also hope the morphing wheels can be used in various applications from autonomous vehicles to military robots.

WHEELS AND AXLES

Inquire & Investigate

DESIGN AND BUILD SIMPLE RACE CARS

The wheel and axle is a simple machine with two parts working together. They rotate together to transfer force from one part to the other. How does the wheel's size affect this simple machine's operation? In this activity, you'll design and build simple race cars and test how they operate with wheels of different sizes.

Ideas for Supplies

- science notebook and pencil
- many buttons of different sizes but with four matching in each size
- twist ties or string
- drinking straws
- ruler
- scissors
- wooden clothespins
- white craft glue or masking tape
- heavy cardboard or similar
- timer (optional)

- **In your science notebook, sketch a design for a clothespin car.** You can explore different designs online at these websites.

- **Select four matching buttons.** These will be the wheels of your clothespin car. Push a twist tie or string through one hole in one of the buttons and thread it back through a second hole so it comes out the other side. Secure the tie or string tightly. Repeat on one of the other buttons.

- **Cut two pieces of a drinking straw measuring 1.5 inches each.**

Good Stuff clothespin car

Crafts Amanda clothespin

Inventors Tomorrow clothespin racer

To investigate more, try adding weight to your cars by taping pennies to the clothespin frame. Repeat the races. Does adding weight affect the car's performance? Explain.

ENGINEERING | CHAPTER SIX

Inquire & Investigate

- **Put the string/twist tie on one button through one piece of straw.** Thread the string/tie to one of the empty buttons at the other end. This creates the car's first axle. Repeat to build the second axle.

- **Open the clothespin and carefully put the straw from one pair of wheels in the clothespin opening.** When you close the clothespin, it should not crush the straw. The twist tie or string inside the straw should still be able to turn freely.

- **Slide the second axle through the other side of the clothespin.** You can secure the axle with white craft glue or a piece of masking tape.

- **Follow the same process to make at least two additional clothespin cars.** Use the same basic car design but vary the size of the button wheels.

- **Set up a piece of heavy cardboard to make a ramp to race your cars.** Before racing, which car do you predict will be the fastest? Which do you predict will travel the farthest?

- **Launch the cars, two at a time, by holding them at the top of the ramp and releasing them.** Were your predictions accurate? Why or why not? How did the size of the wheels affect how the car performed?

VOCAB LAB

Write down what you think each word means. What root words can you find to help you? What does the context of the word tell you?

conveyor belt, diameter, gear, potter's wheel, rolling friction, sliding friction, spoke, waterwheel, wheel, and **winch**

Compare your definitions with those of your friends or classmates. Did you all come up with the same meanings? Turn to the text and glossary if you need help.

TEXT TO WORLD

What wheels beyond tires do you encounter in your daily life?

KEY QUESTIONS

- How have the wheel and axle contributed to human exploration?
- Why do you think the first wheels were used for pottery instead of for transportation?

WHEELS AND AXLES   99

Inquire & Investigate

Ideas for Supplies

- 2 flexible straws
- string
- masking tape
- paper clips
- 2 empty paper towel rolls
- metal washer

To investigate more, adjust your design to increase the size of the crank handle. How does this change how the winch works? Explain.

CRANK A WINCH

A winch is a mechanical device used to wind up or unwind a rope or wire. To use a winch, you turn a crank or handle that rotates a cylinder. The cylinder is attached to a rope or cable that winds up or unwinds depending on the direction of the cylinder's rotation. A winch is based on a wheel and axle. The winch's crank is the wheel, while the cylinder-shaped rod is the axle. In this activity, you'll build a model winch and test how it provides mechanical advantage.

- **Tape one end of a string near the center of one straw.** Tie a paper clip to the other end of the string.

- **Cut two squares out of opposite sides of the tops of each paper towel roll.**

- **Tape the bottoms of the paper towel rolls to a tabletop or countertop, a little less than the length of the straw.**

- **Lay the taped straw across the paper towel rolls so it fits into the grooves you made.**

- **Insert the long end of the second straw into the first straw and bend the tip, so sticks out of the first straw at a 90-degree angle.** Tape to secure it. This is the handle for your crank.

- **Hang a washer on the open paper clip.** Turn the crank to wind the string and raise the washer.

- **Repeat and change where you turn the crank (apply the force).** Does this change the force needed to raise the washer? Explain.

ENGINEERING | CHAPTER SIX

Chapter 7
Putting It All Together

What happens when you combine two or more simple machines?

Compound machines let us create systems that provide even greater mechanical advantage to do harder work.

• • • • • • • •

The six classic simple machines—inclined planes, levers, pulleys, screws, wedges, and wheels and axles—are essential parts of our daily lives. Simple machines make our lives easier, from lifting heavy boxes to riding a bike. They do this by providing a mechanical advantage that allows us to put less effort into getting the job done. If one simple machine can do this, what happens when you combine multiple simple machines? The results can be amazing!

Engineers combine two or more simple machines to create a compound machine. Compound machines provide an even greater mechanical advantage. They can help us tackle bigger and more complex jobs.

Let's take a deeper dive into some of the ways engineers put these six simple machines together to create more powerful machines.

102   ENGINEERING | CHAPTER SEVEN

SCREWS AND LEVERS

A screw is a simple machine that can hold things together. For example, when you screw in a lightbulb or use a screw to keep two pieces of wood together, the screw holds things in place.

As we discussed in Chapter 4, when you turn a screw, you apply a rotational force. The screw turns this rotational force into a linear force that pulls two materials together or pushes them apart. But what if you need help turning the screw? That is where a lever can help. You can use a wrench (lever) to turn the screw more easily.

Have you ever needed to hold a piece of wood completely still while you cut a piece off it? You can use a mechanical tool called a bench vise. A bench vise holds objects firmly in place and is typically attached to a workbench. It has two strong jaws that clamp around an object. You open or close the jaws by turning a handle, which tightens or loosens the grip. People use bench vises in woodworking, metalworking, and other mechanical tasks. Bench vises hold objects securely in place for sawing, drilling, filing, and sanding. They can even hold two parts together while the glue dries.

A bench vise is an example of a compound machine that combines a screw and a lever.

A handle turns the screw, which in turn moves the jaws of the vise closer together or farther apart. This screw changes the direction of the force and increases the force you apply, allowing you to grip objects tightly with less effort.

EFFICIENCY

The efficiency of a machine is a measure of how much work you get out of the machine compared to how much you put into it. Machine efficiency is the ratio of work output to work input. In a perfect world, all the energy put into a simple machine would be converted into useful output or work. The machine would be 100-percent efficient and have no energy loss. However, in the real world, machines always have some energy loss, usually because of friction. Real-world machines always have an efficiency of less than 100 percent. Sometimes, a compound machine has so many moving parts that it produces enough friction to generate heat. To reduce friction, operators may apply lubricants to the machine's moving parts so they slide more easily over each other.

PUTTING IT ALL TOGETHER

The handle acts as a lever. When you turn it, the long handle gives you more rotational force than if you tried to turn the screw by hand. This makes it easier to apply a strong clamping force. The tradeoff, as always, is distance. You'll have to turn the handle (lever) and screw many times to create the force needed to clamp an object in place. But the force will be much less than if you tried to hold the object steady by hand.

The bench vise makes work easier by reducing the force required to grip the object securely. Without the lever, you would need more force to rotate the screw manually. Without the screw, the gripping task would be much more difficult.

FULL STEAM

Some compound machines combine three simple machines, or even more! A wheelbarrow includes a lever, wheels, and inclined planes. A can opener has levers, screws, a wheel, and a wedge!

LEVERS AND PULLEYS

Levers and pulleys go together like peanut butter and jelly. A lever multiplies an applied force using a fulcrum to increase the distance over which the force is applied. As a result, a lever allows you to lift heavier loads with less effort. A pulley changes the direction of a force, allowing you to lift loads by pulling in an opposite or more comfortable direction.

ENGINEERING | CHAPTER SEVEN

Combining a lever and pulley in a compound machine provides the benefits of both simple machines.

A construction crane is one example of a compound machine that uses the lever and pulley together. Construction cranes lift and move very heavy loads. The long arm on the crane, called the boom, acts as a lever. It allows the crane to lift heavy objects with a smaller force. A steel cable connects the boom to the load through a series of sheaves, or pulleys.

Cranes typically use multiple pulleys. The crane's pulley system distributes the weight of the load across several sections of cable and increases the load the crane can lift. In combination, the lever and pulley make it possible to lift and move heavy objects very high into the air.

INCLINED PLANES AND WHEELS

Two simple machines do not always have to be joined together in a compound machine. Sometimes, they can be used individually to make work easier. A good example is inclined planes and wheels and axles working together to move objects more easily.

Have you ever helped moved furniture from one building to another? You might have used a moving van and hand truck. Moving vans have ramps (inclined planes) that make it easier to move heavy objects into the van, even though you have to travel a longer distance. However, as you push a chair up the ramp, friction between the chair and the ramp's surface pushes against your motion.

That's where the wheel and axle can make moving the chair easier. Instead of pushing, what if you pulled the chair on a hand truck?

RUBE GOLDBERG

Rube Goldberg (1883–1970) was an American cartoonist and inventor famous for drawing funny, complicated machines that did simple things. His inventions were called "Rube Goldberg machines." They used many steps and unusual objects to perform easy tasks, such as turning off a light or opening a door. One of his machines might have a toy car rolling down a ramp, hitting a ball, and setting off a series of actions to complete a simple job. Goldberg started as an engineer but loved making people laugh with his silly, creative drawings. He worked for newspapers and magazines, where he made cartoons that made fun of how things could be made too complicated. Today, people still make Rube Goldberg machines for fun, and his name is used to describe any overly complicated way of doing something simple.

PUTTING IT ALL TOGETHER

Watch this video to hear kinetic artist Joseph Herscher talk about building Rube Goldberg machines. **What simple machines can you spot in Herscher's Rube Goldberg contraptions?**

Professional Useless Machine Builder

A hand truck has wheels at the bottom and a platform on which to set heavy things. The wheels reduce friction between the chair and the ramp's surface. By combining these two simple machines—an inclined plane and the wheel and axle—you can move the box up the ramp more efficiently and use less effort than by using either the ramp or wheels alone.

MECHANICAL ADVANTAGE OF COMPOUND MACHINES

Compound machines may be less efficient than simple machines, but they make up for it with their greater mechanical advantage. Each simple machine produces a mechanical advantage. It increases the strength or direction of a force. A compound machine's mechanical advantage is the product of the mechanical advantages of all the simple machines it uses. The greater number of simple machines in the compound machine, the greater its mechanical advantage usually is.

> **FULL STEAM**
>
> Rube Goldberg drew political cartoons as well as his machines. He even won a Pulitzer Prize in 1948!

Let's look at a lever-arm corkscrew. This compound machine is made from two simple machines: the lever and the screw. When you press and turn the screw into the cork in a bottle, the two arms (levers) go up. You then press on the arms to move the cork out of the bottle.

106 ENGINEERING | CHAPTER SEVEN

Let's assume that the mechanical advantage of the levers is 3, and the mechanical advantage of the screw is 2. The mechanical advantage of the corkscrew is the product of the mechanical advantage of the levers and the screw. Therefore, the corkscrew has a mechanical advantage of 6.

$$3 \times 2 = 6$$

What other compound machines can you think of? What simple machines are they made of?

In modern engineering, many tools, vehicles, and machinery use combinations of simple machines. The principles of physics that increase force, change the direction of force, and reduce friction are applied in countless ways to make everyday tasks easier and more efficient. Simple machines have been an important part of life from the earliest days of human history.

The inclined plane, lever, pulley, screw, wedge, and wheel and axle are basic tools that make work more efficient and faster. Today, we use these simple machines every day to help with tasks such as opening doors, lifting boxes, or even playing sports. They are the building blocks of more complex machines, making our work easier and saving time and energy.

Simple machines are everywhere and help us do things better and faster!

KEY QUESTIONS

- Why does mechanical advantage increase when simple machines are combined?
- What combination of simple machines might not increase efficiency?

WEDGES AND LEVERS

What tool do you reach for when you need to cut shapes out of paper? Scissors! A pair of scissors is a compound machine made of wedges and levers. There's a screw in there, too. The handles of your scissors are the effort arms of the levers. The point at which they join is the fulcrum. When you squeeze the handles, you're applying a force that moves the blades together and evenly distributes that force along the wedge, or the sharp edge of the blade. The sharp edge of the blade applies a force to the paper, while the other blade provides pressure in the opposite direction to make a clean cut.

• • • • • • • • •

TEXT TO WORLD

What are some compound machines that you use every day?

PUTTING IT ALL TOGETHER

Inquire & Investigate

DESIGN AND BUILD A RUBE GOLDBERG MACHINE

Rube Goldberg machines often involve multiple steps, with each action triggering the next in a complicated way. For example, a typical Rube Goldberg contraption might start with a ball rolling down a ramp, which might knock over a set of dominoes, resulting in a lever being pulled, and so on, all leading to a very simple goal, such as turning off a light or opening a door. Rube Goldberg machines combine engineering and creativity with a touch of humor.

In this activity, you'll design and build a Rube Goldberg machine using some of the six simple machines.

Ideas for Supplies
- science notebook
- various household materials

- **The first step in the engineering design process is to identify a problem to be solved.** What task do you want to achieve with your machine? Some ideas include turning off a light, crushing a can, or shutting a door.
- **Check out these Rube Goldberg contraptions.** They will give you some good ideas!

Wonderopolis Rube Goldberg

Cool Material Rube Goldberg

DoodleChaos Rube Goldberg

> To investigate more, adjust the design of your machine to include all six simple machines. How does it work? Which simple machines work well together?

108 | ENGINEERING | CHAPTER SEVEN

Inquire & Investigate

- **Next, choose and gather your supplies.** What household items can you use to make your machine? Your items might include:
  - aluminum foil
  - cardboard
  - water bottles
  - paper towel tubes
  - cereal boxes
  - books
  - cans
  - dominoes
  - tape
  - rulers
  - magnets
  - straws
  - craft sticks
  - rubber bands
- **After identifying the problem and gathering the materials you need, sketch a design of your machine.** Incorporate at least three different simple machines in your design.
- **Once the design is complete, begin building the machine.** Test each section before moving on to the next section.
- **Once the machine is complete, test it.** Does it perform as planned? Write down your observations. What parts of the machine worked? What parts did not work? Did it accomplish the intended goal?
- **What changes, if any, can you make to improve the machine's performance?**

VOCAB LAB

Write down what you think each word means. What root words can you find to help you? What does the context of the word tell you?

bench vise, lever-arm corkscrew, and **Rube Goldberg machine**

Compare your definitions with those of your friends or classmates. Did you all come up with the same meanings? Turn to the text and glossary if you need help.

PUTTING IT ALL TOGETHER

GLOSSARY

accessible: able to be used by many people.

agriculture: the practice of farming, including growing crops and raising animals to provide food and other products.

alloy: a mixture of two or more metals or of a metal and another element.

amphitheater: an oval or circular building with rising tiered seats around a central open space or arena.

applied force: a force applied to an object by a person or another object.

aqueduct: a pipe, channel, canal, or bridge built to carry water often over long distances.

arch: a curved structure in the shape of an upside-down U.

archaeologist: a scientist who studies ancient people through the objects they left behind.

Archimedes's screw: a device that moves water from a lower to a higher level.

auger: a tool or device with a screw shaft used to make holes in wood, soil, ice, and other materials.

automate: to operate by machine instead of by human labor.

autonomous: acting independently.

axle: the rod on which a wheel rotates.

balanced force: two forces of equal size acting in opposite directions.

BCE: put after a date, BCE stands for Before Common Era and counts down to zero. CE stands for Common Era and counts up from zero. This book was printed in 2025 CE.

bench vise: device that secures a workpiece, allowing the user to perform tasks such as cutting, drilling, or shaping with precision and stability.

block and tackle: two or more pulleys with a rope or cable threaded between them, usually used to lift or pull heavy loads.

bolt: a strong screw used with a nut to fasten things.

boom: the long, lever-like arm of a construction crane.

bow: the front end of a ship.

caliph: a political and religious leader in Islam.

catapult: a weapon used to throw heavy objects.

chemical energy: energy from a chemical reaction.

chisel: a tool with a flat, sharpened edge used to cut, chip, or shape wood, stone, or metal.

circuit: the complete path traveled by an electric current.

circumference: the distance around the outer edge of a circle.

civil engineering: the branch of engineering that deals with the design, construction, and maintenance of public projects such as bridges, tunnels, roads, and public buildings or spaces.

component: a part of a larger whole, such as a part of a machine.

compound: a substance made up of two or more elements bonded together and not easily separated. Water is a compound.

compound machine: two or more simple machines working together.

compound pulley: a fixed pulley and moveable pulley working together.

concentrate: to make something stronger, denser, or more focused.

convert: to change a material into something else.

conveyor belt: a system that uses a moving band of fabric, rubber, or metal to move objects, often seen in factories or at airports.

cotton gin: a machine that quickly and easily separates cotton fibers from their seeds.

counterweight: a weight that balances another weight.

crop: a plant grown for food or other uses.

cylinder: a hollow tube shape.

diameter: the distance across a circle through the middle.

displacement: the movement of an object from its place or position.

drywall: a building material used to form interior walls and ceilings in buildings.

dumbwaiter: a small elevator used to carry food or other objects between different floors in a building.

durable: able to last.

efficient: wasting as little energy as possible.

effort: the force used on a simple machine to move the load.

ENGINEERING | GLOSSARY

GLOSSARY

effort arm: the part of a lever between the effort and the fulcrum.

elevation: the height of something above sea level.

energy: the ability to do work.

engineer: a person who uses science, math, and creativity to design and build things.

engineering: the use of science, math, and creativity to design and build things.

evolution: the gradual change through time.

first-class lever: a type of lever (such as a seesaw) with the fulcrum in the middle, the load on one end, and the force applied on the other end.

fixed pulley: a pulley joined to a point that does not move.

flint: a very hard, grayish-black rock.

force: a push or pull that changes an object's motion.

fracture: a crack or broken section.

friction: a force that slows down objects when they rub against each other.

fulcrum: the point on which a lever rests or is supported and on which it pivots.

gear: a wheel with teeth around the rim, used in objects to create a mechanical advantage.

gear teeth: the part on a gear that sticks out from the rim and catches on other teeth to move the wheels.

Gothic: a style of architecture used in Europe from the twelfth through sixteenth centuries.

gravity: a force that pulls all objects to the earth.

groove: a line cut into a surface, often made to guide something such as rope along the rim of a wheel in a pulley system.

hieroglyphics: an ancient Egyptian system of writing using pictures and symbols instead of letters or words.

hydraulic: describes a system that pushes and pulls objects using the motion of water or other liquids.

iconic: a widely recognized symbol of a certain time.

inclined plane: a sloped surface that connects a lower level to a higher level.

Industrial Revolution: a period during the eighteenth and nineteenth centuries when large cities and factories began to replace small towns and farming.

innovation: a new invention or way of doing something.

input force: the force used to push or pull an object to make it move or work.

interchangeable: able to be replaced or substituted without making any difference.

inverse: the opposite.

irrational number: a number that cannot be written as a fraction.

irrigation: a system of transporting water through canals or tunnels to water crops.

isthmus: a narrow piece of land that connects two larger pieces of land and is surrounded by water on both sides.

keystone: a wedge-shaped stone that locks the two sections of a Roman arch in place.

lathe: a machine that shapes or cuts materials such as wood or metal by rotating them.

law of conservation of energy: the idea that energy cannot be created or destroyed, just transferred between objects.

leadscrew: a screw used to translate turning motion into linear motion.

lever-arm corkscrew: a tool designed to remove corks from bottles using a screw and two levers.

lever: a simple machine made of a rigid bar that pivots on a support called a fulcrum.

lifting force: a force that lifts in the opposite direction of gravitational pull.

limestone: a kind of rock that forms from the skeletons and shells of sea creatures, used in building construction and cement.

linear motion: movement in a straight line.

load: the object you are moving.

load arm: the part of a lever from the load to the fulcrum.

lock: an engineering feature on canals that helps raise or lower boats from one level of water to another.

loom: a tool used for weaving yarn or thread into fabric.

lubricant: a substance such as oil or grease that reduces friction.

GLOSSARY

machine efficiency: the ratio between the power output of a machine and the power input.

magnitude: size.

mason: a craftsman who builds structures of stone.

mass production: the production of a large quantity of goods, usually by machinery.

matter: what an object is made of. Anything that has weight and takes up space.

mechanical advantage: the amount a machine increases the force to make a task easier.

mechanical energy: energy that uses physical parts you can see, such as the parts of a machine. It is related to motion and height.

mechanics: the working parts of an object or machine.

medieval: a period of time between the fall of the Roman Empire and the Renaissance, roughly between the years 350 and 1450. Also known as the Middle Ages.

mining: taking minerals, such as iron ore, from the ground.

morphing wheel: a wheel with the ability to adjust to the terrain.

moveable pulley: a pulley with one end attached to a fixed point and the other end free to move with the load.

net force: the total of all combined forces acting on an object.

newton: a unit used to measure the amount of force.

normal force: the force pushing upward on an object from the ground.

nut: a small metal fastener with screw threads on the inside, used with a bolt.

onager: a heavy catapult used in ancient times.

ore: a naturally occurring mineral that contains metal.

output force: the amount of force exerted on an object by a simple machine.

papyrus: a form of paper made in ancient Egypt.

parallel: describes objects that run side by side and have an unchanging distance between them.

perpendicular: at a 90-degree angle, called a right angle, to another line, plane, or surface.

pharaoh: the title for ancient Egyptian kings or rulers.

physics: the science of how matter and energy work together.

pi: the number represented by the symbol π and often shortened to 3.14.

pioneer: a person who is among the first to explore or settle a new area.

piston: a short, solid piece of metal that moves up and down inside a cylinder to create motion.

pitch: the distance between the threads in a screw.

pivot: a fixed point that supports something that moves.

plane: a two-dimensional, flat surface with no thickness.

plateau: a flat, raised area of land, higher than the surrounding land.

point: a spot in space or on a line.

potter's wheel: a device with a rotating disc on which clay is shaped into bowls, pots, and other objects.

propeller: a piece of equipment with blades that spin, used for moving a ship or aircraft.

prototype: a working model of something that lets engineers test their idea.

pulley: a wheel, typically with a grooved rim, that a rope or chain is pulled through to help lift a load.

pyramid: a shape with a square base and triangles for sides that meet at a point.

quarry: a pit where stone is cut for building.

radius: the distance from the center of a circle to its edge.

ramp: a sloping surface.

ratio: the relationship in size or quantity between two things.

renewable energy: a form of energy that doesn't get used up, including the energy of the sun and the wind.

revolution: one complete turn made by something moving in a circle around a fixed point.

robotics: the science of designing, building, controlling, and operating robots.

rolling friction: the friction that occurs when an object such as a wheel moves over a surface.

rotate: to turn around a fixed point.

rotational force: a force that causes an object to rotate around a fixed axis.

GLOSSARY

rotational motion: the movement of an object in a circular path.

Rube Goldberg machine: a machine that does a simple task in an overly complicated way in a chain reaction of steps.

screw: a twisted inclined plane wrapped around a rod that pulls one object toward another.

second-class lever: a type of lever, such as a wheelbarrow, with the fulcrum at one end, the load in the middle, and the force applied at the other end.

segment: part of something.

shaduf: a water-lifting device.

shaft: the long narrow part of an object forming the handle of a tool or club

sheave: a pulley.

siege: the process of surrounding and attacking a fortified place, such as a fort, and cutting it off from help and supplies.

simple machine: a mechanical device that changes the strength or direction of a force to make work easier.

sliding friction: the friction between two objects when one object is being moved over another object, such as a box being pushed along the floor.

spoke: a rod or bar that connects the center of a wheel to its outer rim.

standardize: to make one thing the same as others of that type.

steam engine: an engine that burns wood or coal to heat water and create steam. The steam generates power to run the engine.

technology: the tools, methods, and systems used to solve a problem or do work.

terrain: land or ground and all of its physical features, such as hills, rocks, and water.

textile: anything made from fibers or yarns. The fibers can be natural or synthetic.

third-class lever: a type of lever, such as a broom or fishing rod, with the fulcrum at one end, the load on the other end, and the force applied in the middle.

thread: the raised edge that winds around a screw's center.

torque: the amount of force it takes to make something turn or spin.

tradeoff: a giving up of one thing in return for another.

turbine: a device that uses pressure on blades by water, air, or steam to spin generators and create electricity.

unbalanced force: forces of unequal size acting in opposite directions.

vector: a quantity that has magnitude and direction.

waterwheel: a machine that converts the energy of flowing or falling water into energy that can be used to perform a task, such as milling wheat.

wedge: a simple machine that is thick at one end and narrows to a thin edge at the other. It can be used to lift or split another object.

wheel and axle: Used to move items, a circular object and a rod that rotate together when force is applied to one or the other.

wheel: a circular object that can turn on an axle.

whittle: to shape or form by cutting.

winch: a device used to haul or lift something heavy.

wind turbine: an engine fitted with blades that are spun around by the wind to generate electricity.

windmill: a device that converts the energy of the wind to mechanical energy.

work: the amount of energy needed to move an object a certain distance.

METRIC CONVERSIONS

Use this chart to find the metric equivalents to the English measurements in this activity. If you need to know a half measurement, divide by two. If you need to know twice the measurement, multiply by two.

ENGLISH	METRIC	
1 inch	2.5	centimeters
1 foot	30.5	centimeters
1 yard	0.9	meter
1 mile	1.6	kilometers
1 pound	0.5	kilogram
1 teaspoon	5	milliliters
1 tablespoon	15	milliliters
1 cup	237	milliliters

RESOURCES

BOOKS

George, Jennifer, and Zach Umperovitch. *Rube Goldberg's Big Book of Building: Make 25 Machines That Really Work!* Abrams Books for Young Readers, 2024.

Gerencer, Thomas. *How It's Made: The Creation of Everyday Items*. Abrams Books for Young Readers, 2022.

Hays, Brooks Butler. *Makerspace Projects for Building Simple Machines*. PowerKids Press, 2021.

Isogawa, Yoshihito. *The Lego Mindstorms Robot Inventor Idea Book: 128 Simple Machines and Clever Contraptions*. No Starch Press, 2021.

Jacoby, Jenny. *Machines: Technology Is All Around You!* Kingfisher, 2022.

Macaulay, David. *The Way Things Work*. Dorling Kindersley Limited, 2023.

Yasuda, Anita. *Simple Machines! With 25 Science Projects for Kids.* Nomad Press, 2019.

WEBSITES

American Institute of Physics
ww2.aip.org

Kids Discover: Simple Machines
online.kidsdiscover.com/unit/simple-machines

Museum of Science
mos.org

Physics for Engineers and Scientists
wwnorton.com/college/physics/om/_content/_index/tutorials.shtml

Rube Goldberg: About Rube Goldberg
rube-goldberg.com

Science Trek: Simple Machines
sciencetrek.org/topics/simple-machines

Teach Engineering: Simple Machines
teachengineering.org/populartopics/view/simplemachines

The Physics Classroom
physicsclassroom.com

RESOURCES

SELECTED BIBLIOGRAPHY

Brain, Marshall. "How a Block and Tackle Works," HowStuffWorks, accessed July 2025, www.science.howstuffworks.com/transport/engines-equipment/pulley.htm.

"Definition and Mathematics of Work," The Physics Classroom, accessed July 2025, www.physicsclassroom.com/class/energy/lesson-1/definition-and-mathematics-of-work.

Donev, Jason. "Wheel and Axle," Energy Education, accessed July 2025, www.energyeducation.ca/encyclopedia/wheel_and_axle.

Dutfield, Scott, and Jim Lucas. "6 Simple Machines: Making Work Easier," Live Science, February 1, 2022, www.livescience.com/49106-simple-machines.html.

Handwerk, Brian. "The Pyramids at Giza Were Built to Endure an Eternity—But How?" National Geographic, January 21, 2017, www.nationalgeographic.com/history/article/giza-pyramids.

Haskins, Devon. "When a Portland Businessman Patented a New Kind of Screw, It Changed How Quickly Cars Could Be Made," KGW8, November 28, 2023, www.kgw.com/article/travel/whats-in-a-name/portland-businessman-created-phillips-screw-changed-car-manufacturing/283-3e570a9d-fb88-4027-9159-dada09d1d336.

Moul, Russell. "Ancient Technology: How Did the Ancient Egyptians Build the Pyramids?" IFLScience, April 3, 2023, www.iflscience.com/ancient-technology-how-did-the-ancient-egyptians-build-the-pyramids-68208.

"Pyramids: Scaling the Pyramids," Nova Online Adventure, PBS, accessed July 2025, www.pbs.org/wgbh/nova/pyramid/geometry.

Tiner, John Hudson. Exploring the World of Physics: From Simple Machines to Nuclear Energy. New Leaf Publishing Group, 2006.

"What You Don't Know about the Great Pyramid." Stanford Magazine, July/August 2024, www.stanfordmag.org/contents/what-you-don-t-know-about-the-great-pyramid.

RESOURCES

QR CODE GLOSSARY

page 5: pbs.org/wgbh/nova/video/decoding-the-great-pyramid

page 18: nhpbs.pbslearningmedia.org/resource/
phy03.sci.phys.mfw.galileoplane/galileos-inclined-plane

page 20: youtube.com/watch?v=s5AT0XY2Hi0&t=3s

page 35: youtube.com/watch?v=IvUU8joBb1Q

page 36: youtube.com/watch?v=Pj-NqWDH2qE

page 38: youtube.com/watch?v=i5X_jwnb-Ok

page 48: youtube.com/watch?v=pxD3SHMp9Es

page 50: youtube.com/watch?v=8U2BPtYyvW8

page 61: youtube.com/watch?v=h3AfKj37mbo

page 66: youtube.com/watch?v=yzMU8rH4PN8

page 78: youtube.com/watch?v=7ounsxjz17M

page 82: youtube.com/watch?v=O9JdvUw5UZ0

page 90: youtube.com/watch?v=FT_5lICNVtw

page 93: pbs.org/video/design-squad-how-do-bike-gears-work

page 98: youtube.com/watch?app=desktop&v=Ffw88OZr6QQ&t=0s

page 98: craftsbyamanda.com/clothespin-car

page 98: inventorsoftomorrow.com/2016/10/26/clothespin-racer

page 106: youtube.com/watch?v=IWIGo2FOaJk

page 108: wonderopolis.org/wonder/what-is-a-rube-goldberg-machine

page 108: coolmaterial.com/feature/rube-goldberg-machines

page 108: youtube.com/watch?v=6FzUx2EFk8s

INDEX

A

activities (Inquire & Investigate)
- Build a Miniature Aqueduct, 26
- Build a Shaduf to Lift Water, 40
- Build a Simple Lever, 41
- Crank a Winch, 100
- Design a Book Lift, 57
- Design and Build a Catapult, 42–43
- Design and Build a Rube Goldberg Machine, 108–109
- Design and Build Simple Race Cars, 98–99
- Friction on an Inclined Plane, 23
- Investigating Force on an Inclined Plane, 24–25
- Lift a Load with a Pulley, 56
- Lift Water with an Archimedes's Screw, 72–73
- A Screw's Inclined Plane, 74
- The Shape of a Wedge, 85
- Wedges at Work, 84
- Where Are the Simple Machines?, 12
- Which Wedge Works Best?, 86

aerospace industry, 38, 50, 69, 82, 96–97
aqueducts, vi, 16–17, 20, 26
Archimedes/Archimedes's screw, vi, 8, 53, 67, 72–73
augers, 71
axes, vi, 11, 76–77, 80–81
axles. *See* wheels and axles

B

Babbage, Charles, vii
balance scales, 30, 36
bench vises, 103–104
bicycles, 54–55, 89–90, 93
block-and-tackle pulley systems, 53–54
bottle openers, 9, 34
brooms, 35

C

can openers, 104
cars, vii, 9, 11, 22, 38, 65, 69, 88–92, 96–99
carts, wheeled, 88, 90, 94–95
catapults, 8, 36, 42–43
Chinese engineering, vi, vii, 21, 80, 95
chisels, 78, 80, 81
claw hammers, 33
compound machines, 101–109
- definition and description of, 7, 102
- historical use of, vi–vii
- inclined planes and wheels as, 105–106
- levers, wheels and axles as, 7, 34
- levers and pulleys as, 104–105
- levers and screws as, 103–104, 106–107
- levers and wedges as, 7, 33, 107
- mechanical advantage of, 106–107
- Rube Goldberg machines as, vii, 105, 108–109

construction cranes, 104–105
corkscrews, 106–107
counterweights, 37, 47–48, 53
crowbars, 34, 37

D

da Vinci, Leonardo, vi, 52
doorknobs, 91
doorstops, 78, 81
dumbwaiters, 51

E

Edison, Thomas, vii
efficiency, 103
Egyptian engineering, vi, 2–7, 21, 52, 80–81, 95
Eiffel Tower, 52–53
elevators, 46, 53, 55
energy, 9, 103
engineering. *See* simple machines
engineering design process, 7

INDEX 117

INDEX

F

Ferris, George/Ferris wheels, vii
flagpoles, 8, 10, 47
force
    definition of, 19
    friction as (*see* friction)
    gravity as, 19–20, 47, 53
    inclined planes and, 8, 19–20, 23–25
    levers and, 9, 29–32
    mechanical advantage increasing.
      See mechanical advantage
    pulleys and, 8, 46, 50–51
    screws and, 62–66
    torque as, 29, 62
    wedges and, 76–79, 83
    wheels and axles and, 90–94
    work using, 7–9, 15. *See also* work
friction
    compound machines and, 103
    definition of, 19, 66
    inclined planes and, 20, 23
    levers and, 32
    screws and, 65–66
    wedges and, 78, 83
    wheels and axles and, 91–92
fulcrum, 10, 28–35, 37–38, 40–42, 90, 104, 107

G

Galilei, Galileo, 18
gears and chains, vi–vii, 54–55, 92, 93
Goldberg, Rube/Rube Goldberg machines,
    vii, 105–106, 108–109
gravity, 19–20, 47, 53
Great Pyramid, vi, 2–6
Greek engineering, 21, 53, 66–67, 72, 80, 95
Gutenberg, Johannes, vi, 67

H

hammers, 33
Herscher, Joseph, 106
human body, 8, 38–39, 78
Hutchinson, Ayla, 80

I

inclined planes, 13–26. *See also* screws
    current use of, 22
    definition and description of, 10, 14
    force and, 8, 19–20, 23–25
    historical use of, vi–vii, 3–4, 6, 15, 17, 21–22, 26
    how they work, 14–18
    mechanical advantage of, 16–18
    wedges with, 79, 85
    wheels and axles and, 105–106
Indian engineering, vi, 80, 91

J

Jansen, Theo, 36

K

keystones, 83
knives, 82

INDEX

L

law of conservation of energy, 9
leadscrews, 68
levers, 27–43
    current use of, 37–38
    definition and description of, 10, 28
    first-class, 32–33, 38
    force and, 9, 29–32
    friction and, 32
    historical use of, vi–vii, 8, 35–36, 37, 40
    how they work, 29–31
    human body and, 38–39
    mechanical advantage of, 31–32
    pulleys and, 104–105
    screws and, 103–104, 106–107
    second-class, 33–34, 38
    third-class, 35, 38–39, 42
    wedges and, 7, 33, 107
    wheels and axles and, 7, 34
Ljubljana Marshes Wheel, vii, 95
looms, 36

M

machine efficiency, 103
Mason, John Landis/Mason jars, vii, 63
Maudslay, Henry, 68
mechanical advantage
    of compound machines, 106–107
    definition of, 16
    of inclined planes, 16–18
    of levers, 31–32
    of pulleys, 46, 48–51
    of screws, 63–65
    of simple machines, 9, 12
    of wedges, 78–79
    of wheels and axles, 89, 92–94
Mesopotamian engineering, vi, 21, 52, 94
Michelangelo, 81
musical instruments, 35

N

nails, 33, 66, 83
Newton, Isaac, vi, 17
nuts and bolts, 62

O

onagers, 36

P

paddles, 34
Panama Canal, vii, 54
Phillips, Henry/Phillips head screws, vii, 69
pi (π), 64
plows, 77, 81
potter's wheels, vi, 94
primary sources, 4
printing presses, vi, 67
propellers, 69
pulleys, 45–57
    compound systems of, 49–51, 53–54, 105
    current use of, 54–55
    definition and description of, 10, 46
    fixed vs. moveable, 47–48, 53, 56
    force and, 8, 46, 50–51
    historical use of, vi–vii, 8, 51–54, 55
    levers and, 104–105
    mechanical advantage of, 46, 48–51
pyramids, vi, 2–6, 52

R

ramps. *See* inclined planes
Robertson, P.L./Robertson screws, 69
robotics, 38, 52, 97
Roman engineering, vi, 15–17, 20–21,
    26, 36, 53, 55, 80–81, 90, 95
Rube Goldberg machines, vii, 105–106, 108–109

INDEX

S

scales, 30, 36
scientific method, 3
scissors, 10, 33, 107
screwdrivers, 66, 69
screw jacks, 65
screws, 59–74
    Archimedes's, vi, 8, 67, 72–73
    current use of, 70–71
    definition and description of, 11, 60–61
    flathead, 69
    friction and, 65–66
    historical use of, vi–vii, 8, 66–68
    how they work, 61–62
    levers and, 103–104, 106–107
    making of, 68–69
    mechanical advantage of, 63–65
    nuts and bolts vs., 62
    Phillips head, vii, 69
    Robertson, 69
seesaws, 10, 28–29, 32
shadufs, vi, 37–38, 40
shovels, 7, 35
siege ramps, vi, 15
simple machines
    combination of multiple. *See* compound machines
    definition and description of, 6–7
    historical use of, vi–vii, 2–6, 8, 12
    mechanical advantage of. *See*
      mechanical advantage
    types of, 10–11. *See also* inclined planes; levers;
      pulleys; screws; wedges; wheels and axles
    work using, 6–9, 12. *See also* force
spinning wheels, vi, 89, 91
sports equipment, 37, 50, 54, 81
steam engines, vi–vii, 68, 96

T

torque, 29, 62
Trevithick, Richard, vii

W

waterwheels, vi, 95–96
wedges, 75–86
    current use of, 77, 82–83
    definition and description of, 11, 76–77
    historical use of, vi–vii, 80–82
    how they work, 77–78
    levers and, 7, 33, 107
    mechanical advantage of, 78–79
wheelbarrows, vi, 7, 34, 95, 104
wheels and axles, 87–100. *See also* pulleys
    current use of, 90, 96–97
    definition and description of, 11, 88–89
    friction and, 91–92
    historical use of, vi–vii, 91, 94–96
    how they work, 90–91
    inclined planes and, 105–106
    levers and, 7, 34
    mechanical advantage of, 89, 92–94
    shape-changing or morphing, vii, 97
Whitney, Eli, vii
winches, 100
wind turbines/windmills, vi, 91, 95
work. *See also* force
    definition of, 7–8, 15
    efficiency of, 103
    energy for, 9, 103
    simple machines for, 6–9, 12. *See*
      also simple machines
Wright, Orville and Wilbur, 69

Z

ziplines, 48